TROPICAL
MODERN

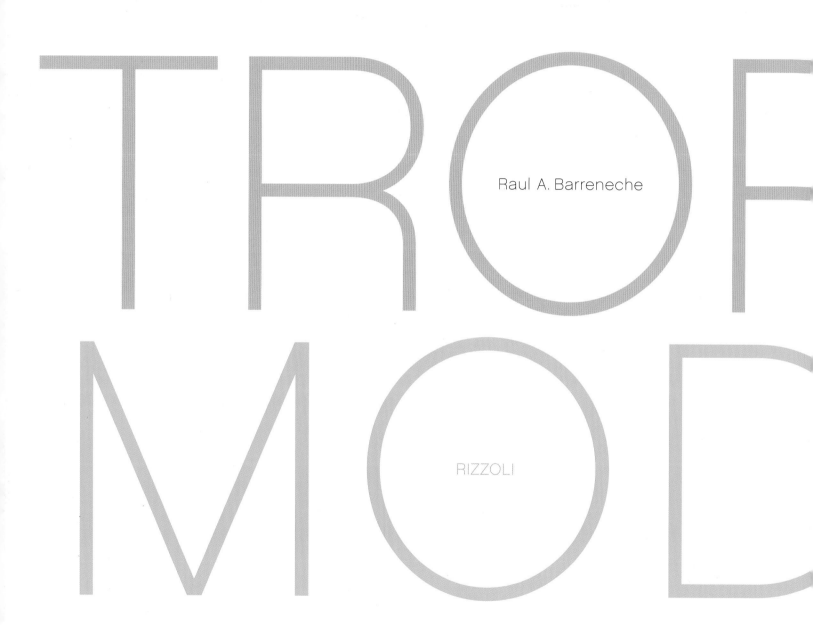

TROP
MOD

Raul A. Barreneche

RIZZOLI

PICAL

ERN

First published in the United States of America in 2003 by
Rizzoli International Publications, Inc. 300 Park Avenue South, New York, NY 10010
www.rizzoliusa.com
© 2003 Rizzoli International Publication, Inc. © 2003 Raul A. Barreneche
2006 2007 2008 2009 2010   10 9 8 7 6 5 4 3 2
ISBN-10: 0-8478-2666-X (HC); 0-8478-2579-5 (PB); ISBN-13: 978-0-8478-2579-0 (PB)
Library of Congress Catalog Control Number: 2003105018
Designed by Claudia Brandenburg, Language Arts; Rizzoli editor: Stephen Case; Copy editor: Octavio Gonzalez
Printed in China

To my parents, for keeping the tropics alive in my childhood imagination; to Jean-Pierre, for showing me how to live a stylish modern life in the tropics; and to all my family who lost their dream homes in Cuba, or who never got to build them. **R.A.B.**

Foreword

As I was finishing this book, a friend asked me whether I was writing about modern houses in the tropics or tropical modern houses. The question stopped me in my tracks. For him, tropical houses are consciously designed around the climate of the tropics, as opposed to houses built in these latitudes whose designs have little to do with the tropical context. He cited the mid-century modern homes designed by German-born architect Henry Klumb in Puerto Rico as innately tropical because they're naturally ventilated, with open-air living rooms and shady dining terraces that seamlessly extend the indoors out. A generic house in the tropics, by comparison, could exist just as easily in the Antilles or Atlanta.

I've always believed that modern houses are naturally suited to the tropics. Great modernist homes like Klumb's celebrate the eternal summer of the tropics—the bright sun, warm breezes, spectacular flora—and minimize the negatives, from the annoyance of high humidity and glaring sun to the damage of heavy rains and deadly hurricanes. Homes less in tune with their environment ignore the pleasures of the tropics as well as the dangers: for instance, sealing off the outdoors with large inoperable windows that become a nightmare in hurricane season, or building with woods that warp in the moist, corrosive atmosphere.

As I thought about my friend's question I realized this is a book about tropical modern houses. I was never interested in publishing houses that just happen to look good next to palm trees or turquoise seas. I wanted to showcase homes with something new to say about modern life in the tropics, in how they deal with climate as well as how they recognize the culture and lifestyle of the region. Needless to say, these houses all exhibit a design sophistication that goes well beyond the tropics: they are on par with the best contemporary houses in the world.

No matter how globalized the world becomes, living in tropical lands is different from living anywhere else. Even in the dead of winter you can pick fresh fruit that seems surreal in its enormous size, odd shape, and vibrant color, rich as that of exotic tropical birds. The humidity can be so intense that crackers go soggy during the course of a few cocktails; writing paper gets moist just from sitting on a table. There can be five minutes of torrential downpours bracketed by hours of brilliant sunshine, or drenching rain for days on end. In both wet and sunny weather women walk along the street with umbrellas. These are the lands of eternal summer, home to some of the most open, generous, and easygoing people on earth.

San Juan, Puerto Rico, January 2003

Houses
Under
the Sun

You can locate the tropics on a map, but they defy simple definition. Technically speaking, the band circling the globe between 23.5 degrees North Latitude (the Tropic of Cancer) and 23.5 degrees South Latitude (the Tropic of Capricorn) marks the boundaries of what can properly be called the tropics. These lines, however, are just invisible geographic guideposts. Within their confines are places that sometimes conform to our mental images of tropical lands and sometimes confound those impressions. There are vast physical differences across this wide swath of the globe, not to mention a huge array of languages and cultures. There are sprawling cities—Singapore and São Paulo, Caracas and Kuala Lumpur—as well as desolate beaches and dense rain forests. There are ecological wonders like the Great Barrier Reef and the Amazon Basin, volcanoes and sandbars, and even sprawling suburbs.

Despite a strong sun and year-round warmth, tropical climate varies greatly. Baja California is a desert, as is Aruba. The north coast of Puerto Rico is humid and green; the south coast, just thirty-five miles away, is arid and brown, with golden mountains that resemble the hills of Southern California. The South Pacific, much of the Caribbean, and both coasts of Mexico are vulnerable to devastating typhoons and hurricanes, while Brazil remains free of tropical storms. There are towering mountains with elevations high enough to turn a hot coastal climate into a cool alpine atmosphere. Mexico City's latitude qualifies it as tropical, but its landlocked perch 7,200 feet above sea level makes for a mild spring all year round, light on oxygen.

The houses featured in this book include beachfront vacation getaways and elegant urban oases; unpretentious, naturally ventilated homes and stylish retreats; colorful houses; and minimalist tropical "lofts." Each responds in its own way to the particulars of place, program, and client, but they share a common vision of tropical living in a modern style. Most of these homes lie deep within the tropical belt, but the projects in Miami, the Bahamas, and the Australian Gold Coast are sub-tropical at best. Still, I've included them because they share the same sensibilities as their counterparts in truly tropical latitudes about living in hot, sunny weather. Tropical is about an attitude and a feeling as much as a geographic location.

Tropical Architecture: The Basics

The basic elements of tropical architecture are more commonsensical than high-tech, gleaned through the centuries from vernacular buildings. The building blocks of houses in the tropics include: naturally cross-ventilated spaces, most likely with louvered doors and windows; properly angled sunshades and eaves that keep the sun at bay; stilts or pilotis that help catch a breeze or avoid flood damage, if necessary; reinforced concrete construction to withstand tropical storms; and steep gabled roofs to shed heavy rainfall.

These time-tested warm-weather design strategies have shaped not only traditional architecture in the tropics but also early modernism in this part of the world. Paul Rudolph started an influential movement with a series of homes designed with Ralph Twitchell around Sarasota, Florida (technically a sub-tropical region) that drew heavily on the local vernacular while establishing a strong modernist vocabulary. Projects like the seminal Cocoon House on Siesta Key (1951) and the Walker Guest House on Sanibel Island (1953) created a modern but climatically appropriate language of wooden louvers that let in the breeze and block out the sun, and raised platforms that cool and protect the house from flooding.[1] The Cocoon House rises up off the sand on footings that create the sensation of a lightweight house barely touching the ground, floating over the water's edge.

In tropical houses like Rudolph's, the barriers between indoors and outdoors are minimal. People live in much closer contact with nature, always in tune with the breeze flowing through an open window or a covered open-air terrace. Rooms don't need any walls at all; hallways and staircases don't have to be enclosed. La Ribereña, a house in Caracas designed by Venezuelan architect Walter James Alcock (page 208), has a luxurious interior circulation of alfresco corridors surrounded by lush tropical gardens. The most liveable rooms have no doors or windows. They're sumptuously furnished indoor-outdoor spaces with sweeping views of the landscape.

Shady, breezy spaces—a must in the tropical summer heat—can be defined with nothing more than grilles and screens, like the sitting room of a house in Singapore by SCDA Architects. This elegant room has no proper skin, just walls of louvered wood doors. When they're closed the doors create the slinkiest of enclosures; when they pivot open, the walls practically disappear, transforming the space into a treetop platform with light filtering in through the slender louvers like sunlight through the wispy fronds of coconut palms.

The Tropical Modern Tradition

Even though modern architecture was born in the cold, gray climate of Bauhaus Germany and de Stijl Holland, it has enjoyed a rich tradition in the tropics. Well into the twentieth century, architects in newly independent tropical countries from Singapore to Sri Lanka to Guyana embraced the neutral character of International Style modernism as a clean break from the neoclassicism of their colonial pasts. Modernism's inherent openness and abstract language made much more sense in the sunlight and warmth of these regions than in the chill of the European continent. Consider Le Corbusier's famous "Five Points." His mandates—pilotis to lift the building off the ground; an open-plan interior; roof gardens; ribbon windows; and a facade independent of the underlying structure—constitute the perfect formula for building in the tropics. To look at the work of Brazilian modern master Oscar Niemeyer is to see the modernist theories of Le Corbusier put into practice, with spectacular results.

In the early 1960s, even before he and Lucio Costa planned the new capital building in Brasília, Niemeyer designed landmark modern houses that adapted Corbusier-influenced European modernism to the tropics. His own home in Rio de Janeiro (1953), known as the Canoas House, is one of the shining examples of tropical modern sensibilities. Niemeyer's home has a fluid, freeform profile with a curving concrete roof that shades the ribbon windows of its undulating facades, as well as terraces that overlook the pool and dense tropical forest. The hinge between the house and the pool is a rocky outcropping that works its way indoors, literally confounding the separation between indoors and out.

In addition to Niemeyer, Brazil produced some of the twentieth century's most brilliant tropical modern houses. Olavo Redig de Campos, who later designed the Brazilian embassy in Washington, D.C., spiked sober rationalism with a dose of sensuality in a home he designed in the Gávea area of Rio (1951). The house mixes streamlined white roof slabs and curving marble-clad volumes, walls of sliding-glass windows that open onto views of Rio's fabled Sugar Loaf, and a tropical garden designed by the great modernist landscape architect Roberto Burle Marx. Like the de Campos house, the House of Glass in São Paulo, designed by often-overlooked Brazilian modernist Lina Bo Bardi in 1951, is a crisp glass box

Vernacular warm-weather design strategies—cross-ventilated spaces; sun shades to keep the sun at bay; and stilts that help catch a breeze or avoid flood waters—helped shape modernism in the tropics.

Paul Rudolph, Cocoon House, Siesta Key, Florida, 1951

Henry Klumb, Fullana Residence, Río Piedras, Puerto Rico, 1955

Oscar Niemeyer, Canoas House, Rio de Janeiro, Brazil, 1953.

that's been "tropicalized." The house is as rational and streamlined as anything designed by Walter Gropius or Mies van der Rohe, but made tropical by letting the lush landscape grow wild around it. Bo Bardi wove the architecture into the surrounding forest, so that hardwood trees climb up through a courtyard and an outdoor staircase rises from a bed of succulents. The living room's de facto wallpaper is a thicket of lush palms viewed through walls of floor-to-ceiling glass. Like Niemeyer's work, these houses reveal the expressive possibilities of tropical modernism: crisp and contemporary, yet warm and sensual.

Outside of Brazil, talented architects throughout the tropics have successfully adapted European modernism to their own climate and culture, from Sri Lanka's celebrated Geoffrey Bawa and Carlos Raul Villanueva in Venezuela to Vladimir Ossipoff in Hawaii and Mario Romañach in pre-Castro Cuba. In Puerto Rico, the architecture of Henry Klumb represents a warmer, more tactile grain of tropical modernism. The German-born Klumb spent five years working with Frank Lloyd Wright before arriving in Puerto Rico in 1944 to head the Committee of Design for Public Works. He fiercely rejected the Spanish revival architecture that vied with International Style modernism as the island government's official aesthetic, calling it "the most wretched [architecture] imaginable."[ii] As an alternative, Klumb proposed a Caribbean take on Wright's Prairie Style, which is evident in his glorious Fullana House outside San Juan. Most of the ground floor of the house, which looks almost exactly the same now as it did when Klumb completed it in 1955, is given over to a large open-air party room enclosed only by carved mahogany grilles. Upstairs, indoor living spaces flow seamlessly outdoors onto a shady dining terrace and a balcony with panoramic views of sea and city.

Foreign architects have also created prominent tropical modernist designs. The California architect John Lautner designed a house perched high on an Acapulco hillside that runs wild with sweeping Niemeyer-style silhouettes and indoor-outdoor spaces. Lautner's landmark Arango house (1973) opens onto views of the Pacific with curving outdoor sitting rooms and terraces sheltered beneath a great freeform concrete roof. A swimming pool snaking along the edge of the terrace completely blurs the line between inside and out, between nature and man-made. In 1955, Italian rationalist Gio Ponti built a masterful villa in Caracas for the Planchart family, with perfectly framed views of towering palm trees and hillsides complemented by stylish interiors filled with Ponti's designs. In 1956, the Austrian-born Richard Neutra designed a stellar home for Alfred de Schulthess in Havana, now the residence of the Swiss ambassador to Cuba. The de Schulthess house reveals Neutra's affinity for healthy outdoor living, an important element of his California houses that really took hold in the warm Cuban climate. Designed with Cuban architects Raúl Alvarez and Enrique Gutiérrez, the home contains large terraces and windows overlooking a lush courtyard garden by Roberto Burle Marx, with swimming pool and a shallow reflecting pool and fountain. Sliding doors along the living room transform the elegant ground-floor into a large terrace overlooking the garden.[iii]

Tropical Living
Weather isn't the only reason the modernist idiom works so well in the tropics. Modernism is also a natural fit with the intangibles of life in the tropics—the casual lifestyle, the quality of light and shadow, and the relaxed, easygoing nature of the people. During a symposium on modern architecture in Latin America organized by the Museum of Modern Art and the New

Lina Bo Bardi, House of Glass, São Paulo, Brazil, 1951.

Olavo Redig de Campos, Moreira Salles House, Rio de Janeiro, Brazil, 1951.

John Lautner, Arango House, Acapulco, Mexico, 1973.

SCD Architects, Coronation Road House, Singapore, 2000.

In the tropics, the barriers between indoors and outdoors are minimal. You can make rooms with no walls at all.

School University, architectural historian Kenneth Frampton remarked on the Brazilian penchant for creating hedonistic spaces.[iv] It's hard to pinpoint what makes space hedonistic, but you can look at the sexy, languid curves of Niemeyer's house and the luxurious open-air rooms of the de Campos house and make the connection between Brazilian modernism and the sensuous, laid-back Brazilian psyche. That same overt sexiness can be seen in the work of the contemporary Brazilian modernist Isay Weinfeld, who designed three houses featured in this book (pages 32, 98, and 188). With their casual elegance, rich palette of local materials, and theatrically scaled interiors, Weinfeld's houses suggest a feeling that's innately Brazilian but also sympathetic with the tropical ethos. Mexican architect Felipe Leal also speaks to hedonistic spaces in a vacation compound he designed in Acapulco (page 42). For Leal, creating pleasure-conscious architecture means exciting all the senses: opening the interiors to spectacular views and plays of light and shadow, and creating sensations of hot and cool with naturally ventilated rooms and plunge pools that flow indoors.

Trends in the Tropics

In writing this book, a few surprising design ideas revealed themselves. Loft spaces, ultimate symbols of gritty urban life, are perfectly suited to the tropics, as much for their breezy, open spaces as for their casual, unprogrammed interiors. Geoffrey Bawa's Jayawardene House, a weekend retreat overlooking the sea in Sri Lanka (page 172), is one such tropical loft. Resembling an empty hangar, most of the house is an enormous viewing platform sheltered by a thin roof and an exposed concrete structure, focused on the sunset over Weligama Bay.[v] Other projects include a home in Baja California designed by LMS Architects, a house by Canadian architect John Hix on Vieques, a trio of houses on Nevis, and a vacation retreat on Australia's Gold Coast—all of which prove the appropriateness of loft living in the tropics.

The sleek minimalism that's been in vogue in recent years also proves to be well suited to the tropics, even if it's a style more readily associated with fashionable boutiques and glamorous uptown apartments. Like Bo Bardi's House of Glass, the neutrality of barely-there minimalist architecture plays off the sunlight and intense colors of the tropics, letting nature take center stage. Among the houses featured in this book, a home in Baja California by New York architect Steven Harris (page 124) and an all-white house by Márcio Kogan in São Paulo (page 136) show that the lush surroundings and bright sunshine of tropical latitudes give minimalism a whole new visual power.

As in other parts of the world, architects in the tropics recognize the importance of designing homes that are environmentally friendly. The powerful sun at these latitudes makes harnessing solar energy a straightforward endeavor. Electricity-generating photovoltaic panels ease the burden of bringing electric lines to remote or "off the grid" sites, as is the case in the house designed by LMS in an isolated corner of Baja California. John Hix's own winter home on the Caribbean island of Vieques minimizes its dependence on local utilities by tapping the sun to power rooftop water heaters and harnessing southeasterly trade winds for natural ventilation. Hix also uses runoff water from showers and sinks to irrigate groves of guava and mango trees surrounding the hillside home. Sydney architects Annabel Lahz and Andrew Nimmo take environmental measures a step further in a house they designed in Australia's Casuarina Beach (page 88). Their crisp modernist design includes a "thermal chimney" that expels hot air; systems to purify rainwater for drinking and wastewater for

Gio Ponti, Villa Planchart, Caracas, Venezuela, 1955.

washing clothes, flushing toilets, and watering the garden; and power-producing photo-voltaic panels. A similar "green modernist" sensibility graces the work of Lahz Nimmo's Australian colleagues Kerry and Lindsay Clare, Andresen O'Gorman, and Bud Brannigan.

There are also designers who tropicalize modernist architecture by mixing local antiques with whitewashed modern spaces, as in Weinfeld's houses; or those that mix indigenous wood and stone with glass and steel, universal signifiers of modern architecture. San Juan architect Maria Rossi, a former designer in the offices of famed architects James Stirling in Berlin and Zaha Hadid in London, designed a house in Caguas, Puerto Rico that hugs its hilltop site with a wall of locally quarried caramel-colored stone. The stone base suggests a traditional building, but the inside of the house is decidedly modern, with an open, airy interior and a double-height living room encased in sliding doors and windows. A dramatic lap pool extends the lean lines of the house outward, pointing assertively towards a view of distant mountains.

The work of these and many other architects around the world proves that there is no single stylistic or conceptual theme dominating contemporary tropical modernism. Urban-flavored loft style, sleek minimalism, environmentally sensitive design, and synthesis of old and new, rustic and sleek are all appropriate strategies for designing houses in the tropics. Of course, none of these categories is a perfect fit. What's certain is that there's no shortage of talented designers building on the legacy of the great tropical modernists. And there is much new ground still left to explore in the future of tropical modern design.

i Bruegmann, Robert. Introduction to Domin, Christopher and Joseph King. *Paul Rudolph: The Florida Houses.* (New York: Princeton Architectural Press, 2002), pp. 15–20.

ii Vivoni Farage, Enrique. "The Architecture of Power: From the Neoclassical to Modernism in the Architecture of Puerto Rico, 1900–1950." Published electronically in ARIS 3: Colonization and Architecture by the Department of Architecture, Carnegie Mellon University.

iii Rodriguez, Eduardo Luis. *The Havana Guide: Modern Architecture 1925–1965.* (New York: Princeton Architectural Press, 2000.) pp. 54–55.

iv Comments made at symposium, October 11, 2002.

v *Modernity and Community: Architecture and the Islamic World.* (London and Geneva: Thames & Hudson, Ltd. and the Aga Khan Award for Architecture, 2001) p. 33.

Richard Neutra, de Schultess Residence, Havana, Cuba, 1956.

Maria Rossi, Caguas House, Caguas, Puerto Rico, 2000.

Projects

Isay Weinfeld, architect

Altério Residence
São Paulo Brazil

São Paulo architect Isay Weinfeld is a master of designing sleek minimalist spaces infused with rustic Brazilian materials and furnishings. He can pair eighteenth-century tables and dressers from Bahia with mid-century modern chairs in an all-white space to create a sexy, elegant interior that works seamlessly. He also knows how to manipulate scale to make dramatic theatrical spaces that surprise and delight with their sheer size.

Weinfeld designed a house in São Paulo's lush Jardim Europa district for Brazilian music impresario Fernando Altério that captures the essence of the architect's unique take on timeless modernism in the tropics. The house turns a solid face to the street—mostly for security reasons, as evidenced by a small built-in guardhouse tucked discretely off to one side of a slatted aluminum wall. Behind the wall, the house appears as a solid brick box with a tiny Corten-steel balcony peering over the wall like a one-eyed sentinel. Passing through the guarded entry gate, the path leading to the front door keeps up the air of mystery and seclusion. As Weinfeld explains, "As in all my work, the house doesn't tell you the whole story when you enter. There's an element of surprise. You don't know where you're going."

Just inside, however, the house starts to loosen up. A powder room off the foyer pairs a rough wood counter with a travertine sink and gilded Baroque wall sconces dripping with crystals. The big architectural surprise awaits at the back of the house: a soaring 23-foot-tall living and dining room with a wall of glass doors that slide open to make an almost outdoor room open onto a lush garden. There are two seating areas on either side of the dining room, with a mix of custom travertine side tables, 1940s French lamps, and chairs by Brazilian mid-century modern designers. In this space, the owner likes to throw huge dinner parties after concerts at one of his music halls. You can imagine a sexy soiree spilling out into the garden on a warm night, with Brazilian jazz wafting through the space and the sound of water from a small fountain outside animating the evening. For more formal sit-down entertaining, Weinfeld designed a dining room set into a mirrored recess framed by a large wall at the back of the soaring space. With its dramatic proportions, the wall resembles a proscenium arch, with the dinner party as the on-stage attraction.

Upstairs are the private quarters. Sliding wood doors screen the master bedroom that sits on axis with the symmetrical living space. There's a spacious study off to one side of the bedroom and a large dressing area and bathroom to the other. Behind the master suite are identical bedrooms for the owner's two daughters, with separate bathrooms and a shared balcony over-looking the street. The third floor has a glass pavilion enclosing a spacious gym and steam room, surrounded by a deck with panoramic views of Jardim Europa's leafy streets and São Paulo's *Blade Runner* sprawl all around. As in the living room, glass doors wrapping the gym slide open to create a virtual outdoor room in the treetops.

Weinfeld's strategy of keeping the house closed to the street and open at the back let him create a lush tropical space in the middle of this vast, crowded city. And the giant glass doors do away with rigid divisions between indoors and outdoors; even on a rainy day, sitting in the living room makes you feel like you're part of the palm-filled courtyard just outside. Even though it's a sophisticated, elegant urban house geared towards entertaining on a grand scale it's laid back and casual—and very tropical.

Tucked behind a slatted aluminum wall, the home's streetside elevation is boxy and spare, clad in stucco and brick with a weathered steel balcony.
Following spread: Day and night, the soaring living room opens up with 21-foot-tall glass doors to create a vast indoor-outdoor space, with an archway framing the dining room like a giant stage set.

Above left: A wall of smooth pebbles makes a textured backdrop to a lap pool in the private garden.
Above right: Glass doors slide open to create an alfresco rooftop gym with views of São Paulo's leafy Jardim Europa neighborhood.
Facing page: The dining room features wood chairs by the Brazilian mid-century designer Sergio Rodrigues.
Following spread: Sliding wood doors screen the master suite from a balcony overlooking the living room.

Ground floor plan

Second floor plan

Third floor plan

Felipe Leal, architect

Casas La Chiripa
Acapulco Mexico

Mexico City architect Felipe Leal designed two adjoining vacation houses—one for himself—perched high above a cliff overlooking the Pacific in the heart of Acapulco, where Errol Flynn, John Wayne, and the Rat Pack vacationed in the 1940s and 50s. Leal's houses straddle a steep rocky outcropping known as "La Mira," one of the dramatic cliffs that encircle Acapulco Bay, almost 300 feet above the sea. From this scenic perch, the vacation homes enjoy spectacular views of the water and the city, as well as cool breezes that make air conditioning unnecessary.

The houses resemble a series of stacked viewing platforms, oriented to offer postcard-perfect views. "The setting made me create architecture for the senses—a hedonistic space," says Leal.

From street level at the top of the hill, the two houses look like modest three-story buildings, one finished in smooth white stucco with wooden jalousie windows, the other veiled with a slatted wood screen. Seen from the water, however, they reveal themselves as delicate five-story structures, interconnected but independent. While the street-side facades are somewhat severe, the waterside elevations are delicate and almost ephemeral, with sliding glass doors—sometimes no doors at all—and slender steel columns supporting wooden sunshades like the masts of a sailboat. Wooden decks at various levels lend the houses a nautical air. Leal says the docks, piers, and covered gangways of the nearby port inspired his choice of materials.

The house to the east contains an open, loft-like living-dining space and a kitchen on the ground floor. The living-dining area has windows on the west wall but no enclosure to the south. The cobalt blue-tiled swimming pool flows indoors, drawing one's view straight out to the ocean. Above the living area is a bedroom pavilion with sliding-glass doors that create a windowless sleeping aerie with seaside views. Delicate steel columns supporting the slatted wood screen above the bedroom deck plunge down several stories to the edge of the pool. Directly below the pool is another bedroom suite, reached by an outdoor staircase winding down the cliff.

On the bay side, the westernmost house is skewed from its neighbor for a slightly different orientation; a slatted wooden wall between the two lends extra privacy. On the ground floor, the second house contains living and dining areas, with an open kitchen. Down the hill is another terrace with a patch of lawn and its own private pool at the bottom of the cliff.

Leal paid careful attention to the placement of doors and windows to generate cross-ventilation and make air-conditioning unnecessary. As Leal says, "It would be absurd not to take advantage of the benefits of the site." Slatted wood screens create shade and privacy while letting the breezes flow. Ceiling fans give a boost to the natural air circulation.

With their minimalist quality, Leal's houses open up sensory experiences in a spectacular setting. Leal says his objectives were to let visitors "hear the sounds of the ocean, tropical birds, and the wind; refresh themselves in the pool; be bathed by the sun and the water, surrounded by modernity and austerity. This helps them understand how nature behaves and lets them experience directly the reality of the tropics."

Seen from the hilltop entry road, the adjoining houses have two distinct identities. One is wrapped in a slatted wood screen, its neighbor in smooth white plaster.

Section through hillside

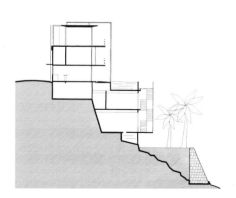

Entry elevation

Above left: Slender steel columns supporting a wooden sun shade resemble the masts of a sailboat.
Above right: Wooden decks with spectacular views of Acapulco Bay also give the neighboring houses a nautical air.
Facing page: The terraces of the two houses are slightly skewed and the pools placed on different levels to create privacy without sacrificing views.

Entry level plan

Lower level plan

Second floor plan

The pool of the wood-clad house flows inside the dining room, completely blurring the boundaries between indoors and outdoors. **Facing page:** Sliding glass doors at the corner of the top-floor bedroom create an open-air sleeping perch shaded by a slatted wood screen.

Keenen/Riley, architects

Palm Island House

Miami Beach
Florida
U.S.A.

Talk about the transformative power of design: Architect John Keenen of the Manhattan firm Keenen/Riley turned a nondescript 1950s house in a gated island community in Miami's Biscayne Bay into a spectacular, sophisticated home filled with exceptional contemporary furniture and art. Commissioned by a prominent businessman and art collector but since sold, the project was no simple remodel: Keenen turned a four-bedroom house into a luxurious one-bedroom home (plus guestroom), demolishing an entire bedroom and service wing and refinishing "every single surface in the house," by his estimate. Tearing down the L-shaped wing that extended from the kitchen towards the street and defined a frame for the front yard changed the entire disposition of the house and allowed Keenen to create a lush new entry.

The reconfigured house has two completely different personalities. The entrance side is shady and mysterious, with a path of concrete pavers leading through a dense grove of towering bamboo, part of a superb plan by renowned landscape designer Edwina von Gal. The pavers cross over a narrow moat and continue right up to the front door. Instantly, the moody world of the bamboo entry garden gives way to a bright interior of sparkling materials and top-notch modern furniture and design.

The ground floor contains a guestroom, kitchen, and an open living and dining room. Sliding doors between the living room's curving, mosaic-covered piers open onto an angular pool and a lawn dotted with palm trees, overlooking Biscayne Bay. A structurally daring staircase—cantilevered "vertebrae" of terrazzo steps supported by a stainless-steel "spine"— leads up to the spacious master suite. At the heart of this plush, luxurious retreat is an oval-shaped walnut shell inspired by Mies van der Rohe's iconic Tugendhat House. The curving wood wall partially encloses the master bath, covered in tiny ceramic tiles and a curving glass wall shielding the shower. Translucent sliding-glass doors beyond the shower reveal the bamboo grove outside, creating the effect of bathing in the treetops. Adjoining the bedroom are a study, dressing area, and roof deck with views of the bay and the downtown Miami and Miami Beach skylines.

Keenen resurfaced the first floor exterior in white stucco and the upstairs in vertical slats of cedar siding stained pale gray to recall Pietra Serena stone. Inside, he set a cool color palette with gray terrazzo floors, whitewashed walls, and chunky columns covered in tiny ceramic tiles. The materials' colors and textures create a luminous background for the light reflected off the bay and into the house through large sliding-glass doors. Furnishings are a mix of custom pieces by Keenen/Riley, and others designed by modern masters Robsjohn-Gibbings, Ico Parisi, and Franco Albini. The art is even more memorable: work by, among other artists, Mark Morrisroe, Ross Bleckner, and Ed Ruscha, whose vivid *Screaming in Spanish* guides your view up the open staircase.

The house embodies elegant warm-weather living at its scintillating, dressed-up best; but there's an easy, casual quality about it. "The layout, with an open living and dining room, and the openness of the stair keep it informal, even though the furnishings and the art are all pedigreed," explains Keenen. "Materials like terrazzo, and a strong indoor-outdoor relationship, make the house feel 'tropical.' But ultimately it's the light and the water that really make it tropical."

The back side of the house overlooks a sunny lawn dotted with towering palm trees. Large sliding glass doors wrap the living-dining room, beneath a roof deck adjoining the full-floor master suite.
Following pages: Large windows and light materials make the living room (right) and master suite (left) feel bright and airy.

Materials like terrazzo and tile, a strong indoor-outdoor relationship, and the sunlight and water really make the house tropical.
—John Keenen

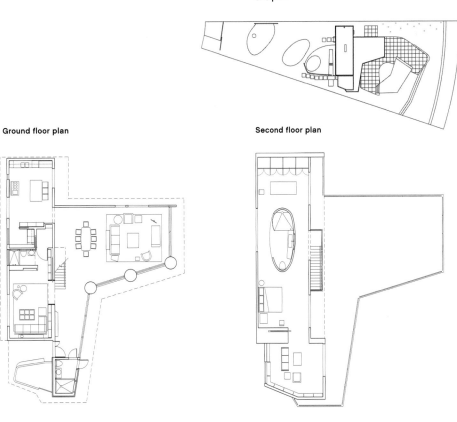

Site plan

Ground floor plan

Second floor plan

The interiors are filled with collections of mid-century and contemporary furniture and art by the likes of Ross Bleckner (top left) and Ed Ruscha (top right).
Following pages: Thickets of dense bamboo create shady outdoor rooms along the entry path.

Frank Harmon Architect

Taylor House
Scotland Cay Bahamas

The more than 700 tiny coral islands that make up the Bahamas have some of the most spectacularly clear turquoise water and white sand beaches anywhere. Unfortunately, their small size makes these charming islands especially vulnerable to spontaneous storms and well-formed hurricanes. Scotland Cay in the Bahamas' Abacos chain reveals yet another dark side of this paradise: scorpions, mosquitoes, and the toxic leaves of the aptly named poisonwood tree. It has the added inconvenience of no potable water supply. There are only about sixty houses on the mile-long island, accessible via a tiny harbor or an airstrip.

Undeterred by the constraints of building on this rustic tropical outpost, the late Raleigh, North Carolina–based industrial designer Jim Taylor and his wife Janice decided to construct their vacation house on Scotland Cay. The Taylors hired Raleigh architect Frank Harmon, an alumnus of Richard Meier's New York office, to design the house, asking him to create a "tent pitched in paradise," or a "sea-hawk's nest overlooking the sea." The architect complied by designing a simple modern structure that rises three stories above a dense thatch of mahogany and gumbo limbo trees, on a coral ridge thirty feet above the sea.

Harmon literally turned the traditional Bahamas house on its head: He inverted the typical pitched wooden roof, creating a giant umbrella over a concrete box. At the center of the wooden umbrella is a large drain that catches rainwater and funnels it into a pair of 8,000-gallon cisterns on the ground floor. As it flares upward and out, the roof directs cooling breezes into the open third-floor living spaces, shading the interior with its deep overhang. Harmon engineered the roof, finished in marine plywood, to resist 120 M.P.H. winds. Steel beams connect the roof to four reinforced concrete columns, which in turn are anchored to the foundations "like chin straps on a hat."

The height of the house not only gave the Taylors a 360-degree view out over the water on the top floors, but also put them well above the mosquito-filled scrub forest. On the third floor are the kitchen and an open living-dining room tucked beneath the umbrella roof. Roughly half of the third level is enclosed; the rest is a pair of outdoor decks facing the ocean. The second level, more sheltered than the top floor, contains a pair of bedrooms with a shared bathroom, another outdoor deck with an open-air shower, and a screened-in sleeping porch. The large cisterns share the ground floor with a workshop space.

Harmon devised a series of enclosures to secure the Taylors' house during hurricanes, and while they are away from the Bahamas. Painted in a Caribbean palette of pale blues and bright reds, the sometimes quirky flaps and shutters animate the home's simple stucco-covered concrete facade, giving the house a playful personality. The living room features a flip-up shutter made of marine plywood with an aluminum tube frame held open by nylon cords hooked into the cantilevered roof. A rolling plywood shutter, similar to a barn door, shields the second-floor bedrooms; two little red windows set into the door align with the bathroom windows when the door is rolled away from the bedroom. Harmon later added a rolling aluminum shutter and half-inch-thick Plexiglas to shield the living space.

Understanding the limitations of the home's isolated location, Harmon kept the building materials to easily obtainable stucco, marine plywood, and reinforced concrete blocks. Steel

Right: A giant inverted roof sheathed in wood shelters the boxy three-story house. **Far right:** Colorful shutters and sliding doors provide shade as well as protection from hurricanes.

to reinforce the roof had to be shipped from Miami. The owners hired a Norwegian contractor and former ship engineer from nearby Abaco Island to build the house, and an intern from Harmon's office spent weeks helping to build the complex roof, shutters, and flaps.

So far, the house has withstood several major storms, including Hurricane Floyd in 1999, which whipped the Bahamas with 150 M.P.H. winds. Harmon's design for a sturdy, self-sufficient building paid off. After Hurricane Floyd, the Taylors were the only ones on Scotland Cay with cisterns full of water. But in addition to its toughness, the Taylor House has an open, easygoing character perfectly suited to its tropical setting. It's also a sophisticated little building—a comfortable loft by the sea.

Top floor plan

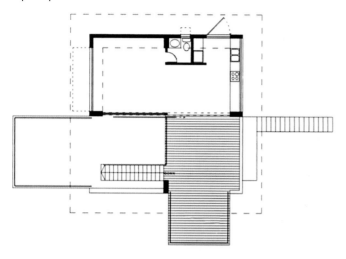

Entry level plan

Right: A roomy deck adjoining the second-floor bedrooms functions like a spacious outdoor living room sheltered by the inverted wooden roof. **Far right:** Stairs leading up from the second-floor deck to a dining terrace and indoor living room pass a framed view of the Bahamas' turquoise sea.

Diagram of rainwater collection and natural ventilation

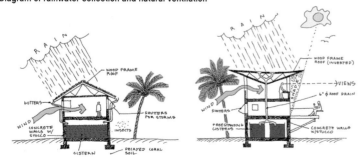

TRADITIONAL BAHAMAS HOUSE

Exploded axonometric diagram

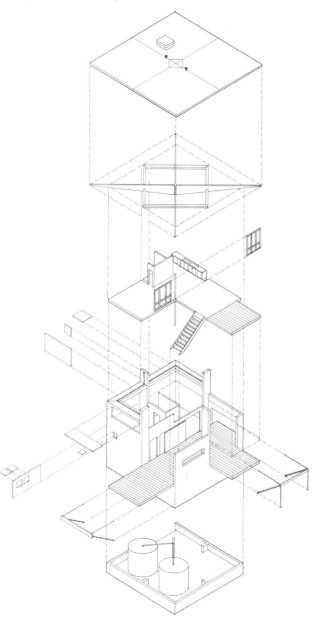

The main terrace offers
views of the tropical
sunset while lounging or
showering al fresco.

Visual surprise is natural in the Caribbean; it comes with the landscape, and faced with its beauty, the sigh of History dissolves.
—Derek Walcott, Nobel laureate

Henry Myerberg, architect

Casa de Crystal

Vieques Puerto Rico

On the unspoiled Caribbean island of Vieques, just off the eastern coast of Puerto Rico, New York architect Henry Myerberg designed a light, breezy vacation home for a Manhattan dealer of twentieth-century furniture. The original client has since sold the house, but the suitability of Myerberg's original design remains: he drew inspiration from the furniture and structural designs of French architect Jean Prouvé, a perfect source for a client who sold Prouvé furniture.

The structural solution is quite simple: a pair of two-story wishbone- or Y-shaped concrete piers supports a flat concrete roof sheltering a glass box like a giant concrete umbrella. Freed from the task of supporting the roof, the skin becomes open and light, with a simple grid of concrete piers spanned by sliding-glass doors wrapping a wide-open interior. (The wishbone piers don't do all the structural work: round concrete columns placed just inside the window walls also help support the roof.) The thin profile of the aluminum door and window frames, and frameless glass corner windows make the skin feel delicate and almost nonexistent. Although the giant Y-shaped piers and spacious interiors give the house a strong identity, they play a supporting role to the tropical sunlight and spectacular views that fill wall-to-wall windows in every room.

A long side of the glass box faces southeast, towards a view of the Caribbean, the same direction as prevailing trade winds. Surrounded by green hills, views of the house are obscured from the access road; you can't see the house until arriving at the entry gate. The vast double-height living room, dining area, and kitchen are on the ground floor; a laundry room and bathroom with shower are reachable only from an outdoor deck. Sliding doors partially define all four sides of the ground floor, opening onto a terrace finished in the same terra-cotta tiles found inside the house—creating the illusion of an interior floor that extends outdoors. Upstairs are a guestroom with separate bathroom and a master suite overlooking the pool deck. From the beds both bedrooms enjoy dramatic views of the sunrise over the Caribbean and two islands just offshore, an especially inspiring way to greet the day.

The house sits atop a pale gray concrete podium that conceals huge cisterns, lifting the house high above the trees, like the base of a classical temple. Myerberg designed the recently added pool deck as a second plinth, this one concealing an extensive gym, bathroom, and storage space. According to Myerberg, the podiums are riffs on Prouvé's designs for structures anchored to floating platforms. Another source of inspiration was El Fortín, a

Walls of sliding glass doors in the airy double-height living room open onto views of the Caribbean. A curving staircase winds up to the bedrooms.

tiny colonial Spanish fort on Vieques. Long wooden benches wrap the length of the plinth-decks, giving these outdoor areas definition and continuity.

To keep the trade winds flowing through the second floor, Myerberg kept the interior partition walls low enough to facilitate cross-ventilation through the operable clerestory windows. In the master bedroom, the closets and bathroom don't extend the full height of the ceiling; neither do the walls of the guestroom and guest bathroom. To allow for greater air circulation, there is a compromise in acoustical privacy. The huge open volume of the house and the lack of soft surfaces compound the acoustical complications. But that openness keeps the interior breezy, informal, and perfectly attuned to sun, breezes, and panoramic views.

Given the limited materials available in Vieques, where nearly everything, from gasoline to groceries, is shipped from Puerto Rico by ferry, Myerberg stuck with a simple palette: poured concrete, stucco-covered concrete block, and tile. The sliding-glass doors were imported from the US mainland; the steel staircase was made in the Berkshires of Massachusetts and shipped to the island. The entire house has "a Prouvé look built with Vieques technology," suggests Myerberg. It's sophisticated enough to make for a sybaritic escape, but suitably casual for this carefree tropical island.

Second-floor plan

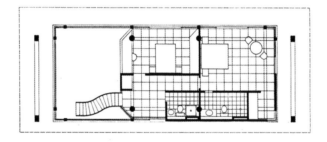

One of the home's distinctive features—one of two Y-shaped concrete piers based on the designs of Jean Prouvé—is visible through a wall of floor-to-ceiling glass. The furnishings are a mix of mid-century classics.

Ground-floor plan

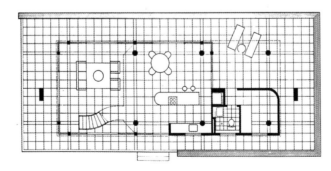

Leddy Maytum Stacy Architects

Casa de Carmen

Rancho Nuevo Mexico

Carmen Gutierrez and Rodney Bradley needed an escape from harsh Alaska winters, so they asked San Francisco architects Leddy Maytum Stacy (LMS) to design a getaway on a remote desert site along the coast of southern Baja California. The couple eventually made their winter home their primary residence, trading in the tundra for views of the Pacific Ocean from a 20-foot bluff overlooking the beach. The site is remote, miles from the nearest town and so far off the utility grid that the house had to generate its own electricity with photovoltaic panels.

LMS designed what they call a modern interpretation of Mexican vernacular architecture: a fresh take on the strong forms, saturated colors, and flowing outdoor spaces that mark traditional Mexican architecture. Modern architect Luis Barragán made this kind of rich, colorful minimalism his trademark; Barragán disciple Ricardo Legorreta brings this bold Technicolor architecture into the present with a postmodern edge.

Although it has occasional echoes of Barragán, LMS's design is original and unencumbered by the clichés of Mexican modernism. They created a loft-like home with colored plaster and native materials, including local stone, deep-blue mosaics, bright-red tiles, and plenty of outdoor rooms in which to enjoy the warm, dry climate of this tropical desert.

The entrance to the concrete house is through a slatted wood gate set into a colored plaster wall, with stone steps rising up from the stark desert landscape. Once inside the gate, the house unfolds as a series of separate volumes with indoor and outdoor rooms directed towards the ocean. The stone entry path passes a row of gardens dotted with native desert plants, past an allee of palms to the front door. A roofless tower marks the entrance, with a second-floor lookout that bears the indelible imprint of Barragán: a vibrant corner cutout in the red stucco walls frames a glimpse of blue ocean in a surrealistic composition.

The main living space is an open loft-like volume divided roughly into thirds by a dining room, living room, and free-flowing kitchen. Sliding doors on the west side of the living area open onto a covered terrace with ocean views. A door on the south side of the kitchen opens onto another covered terrace with a built-in concrete table and benches for outdoor dining. The dining terrace wraps around this side of the house and flows into an open courtyard—a modern take on traditional Mexican patios—where a built-in sink, grill, and fireplace make outdoor entertaining easy. The courtyard separates the main living areas from a freestanding pavilion, which houses a guestroom and study with a shared bathroom. The guestroom and study open onto a shared veranda off the garage.

With their second-floor master suite reached via a narrow staircase off the kitchen, Gutierrez and Bradley maintain total privacy. From this self-contained aerie high above the beach, the couple enjoys spectacular views from their platform bed and from an elevated tub surrounded by windows on both sides.

Casa de Carmen illustrates how modern architecture can facilitate carefree living in the tropics. Bringing the idea of an open loft to the beach does away with the formality of strictly defined rooms. After all, who wants anything other than casual living in a beach house?

The colorful house sits high on a bluff overlooking the Pacific Ocean in a remote corner of Baja California. **Following pages:** The sequence into the house leads visitors through a wooden gate in the stucco entry wall, through a courtyard landscaped with cactus and other desert blooms, and down a walkway paved in native stone. A cantilevered staircase along a tiled wall (far right) leads to a rooftop sitting area.

This loftlike home with colorful plaster walls and native stone and tile has spacious outdoor rooms in which to enjoy the warm, dry climate of this patch of tropical desert.

A quiet outdoor room wrapped in bright-red stucco walls frames a view of the Pacific Ocean.
Following pages:
A bright tile wall marks the open kitchen and dining area (left). The bed and bath in the master suite (right) are lifted up for lounging with a view.

Floor plans

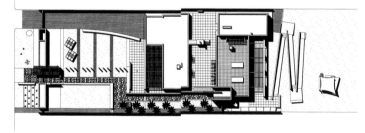

Section through site

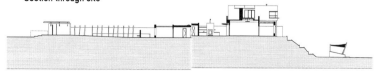

Beach House Casuarina Beach Australia

I sought the curved and sensual line. The curve that I see in the Brazilian hills, in the body of a loved one, in the clouds in the sky and in the ocean waves.—Oscar Niemeyer, Brazilian architect

Isay Weinfeld, architect

Sverner Residence
São Paulo
Brazil

Like the house he designed on nearby Rua Suíça (p. 32), this house by architect Isay Weinfeld on Rua Inglaterra turns a solid face to the street, saving the views for the more secure rear yard. In this home, the guardhouse is even more discreet: a narrow translucent window set into a wall of horizontal pine siding at the end of a stucco wall. Except for another caramel-colored pine tower, which Weinfeld chose because of its "very strong personality," the entire exterior of the home is a cool composition of white volumes.

Once through the gate, however, architectural surprises abound. The closed entry facade gives way to a luminous whitewashed courtyard, with a gravel path shaping a shallow pool filled with enormous river stones in a game of contrasting scales. Polished blue-white rocks—resembling smooth, shiny pebbles blown up on a color copier—compete for attention with stalks of twisting, sculptural bamboo peeking through a cutout canopy. The water is a concession to the client, who didn't want a swimming pool but still wanted to hear the sound of water.

Inside, the L-shaped house continues Weinfeld's skillful mix of serene spaces with rich Brazilian materials bathed in light. A hallway finished in the same dark ipé wood flooring used throughout the house, ending with sliding-glass doors that open onto a grassy courtyard, lines the length of the L-shape. Door frames are made from the same honey-hued pine Weinfeld used in the exterior. Elsewhere, the use of such different wood materials might be jarring, but here it is deliberate: Weinfeld matched the ipé floors to the color of the dark brown knots in the pine. When the doors slide open, white curtains rustle along the length of the hallway, adding another color and texture to the space. The hallway leads into the open living and dining areas, ending in an outdoor dining terrace with trees peeking out from the louvered clerestory wrapping the deck. The short end of the L-shape contains an office with views of the lawn and garden.

Upstairs, another hallway extending the length of the L leads to three bedrooms and a family room. Along this corridor, Weinfeld created a spectacular wall of stacked Brazilian arenite stone, bathed in sunlight from a sliver of skylight extending the entire length of the wall. The rough stone wall, which looks more like an outdoor-garden wall than an interior surface, glows against the dark ipé floor. At the end of the hall, the master suite contains a cool, luxurious bathroom finished in white marble with streaks of gold, called Macchia Oro.

The house contrasts sleek modern elements—Mies van der Rohe's Barcelona chairs, a Donald Judd–like stainless-steel firewood holder—and rustic pieces like an eighteenth-century Brazilian hall table, cow-skin rugs, and rough, imperfectly textured pine and stone. Its strong modern elements make the house sophisticated for its big-city setting; native Brazilian materials, expertly finished and carefully chosen, as well as its open-air, outdoorsy feel, keep the home firmly rooted in the tropical tradition.

The second-floor bedroom wing, covered in slatted pine louvers, overlooks a private garden at the rear of the house.

The street façade
is a cool composition
of stout volumes
finished in stucco and
golden pine.
Right: The entry court
features a dramatic
play of light and scale,
with a pathway winding
past a pool of smooth
white river stones.

Water flowing into the stone-filled pool creates a soothing sound in the entry court.
Above right: Like the courtyard, the foyer creates a serene mood with whitewashed walls bathed in natural light.

Ground floor plan

Second floor plan

When the doors
slide open, billowy white
curtains rustle along
the length of the hallway,
introducing another
color and texture into
the space.

The formal living room
becomes an indoor-
outdoor space
overlooking the quiet
backyard garden
when wood-framed
glass doors slide open.
Following pages:
The interiors feature a
mix of warm native
Brazilian materials
including a second-floor
hallway with a light-
washed wall of arenite
stone (far right).

Studio MORSA, architects

Three Houses by Studio MORSA
Nevis West Indies

Antonio Morello and Donato Savoie of Studio MORSA may best be known among Manhattan's fashionable set as the architects of the landmark SoHo restaurant Barolo and the futuristic Comme des Garçons store in Chelsea, which they designed in collaboration with fashion designer Rei Kawakubo, Japanese architect Takao Kawasaki, and Future Systems of London. Far from the crowded sidewalks and concrete canyons of New York City, Morello and Savoie designed the three houses on the tiny Caribbean island of Nevis, one of the lush sister islands comprising the former British colony of St. Kitts and Nevis, with a startling palette of rich tropical colors: saturated blues, deep reds, and bright yellows. In fact, the architects like to refer to the houses, perched on nearby hillside lots 1,200 feet above the sea, as "parrots in the jungle."

Studio MORSA's bold color scheme started innocently enough: They wanted houses with red rooftops, a symbol of welcome and hospitality on many Caribbean islands and especially Nevis, where African inhabitants traditionally painted their roofs red to keep evil spirits at bay. From there, the idea took flight. "We thought about how great it would be to look up and see patches of colors against the green mountains," Morello explains. "We never wanted to do a carnival of architecture or buildings that didn't belong to the forest, but something appropriate for this island."

Adds Savoie, "We wanted the houses to be cool, dark, but colorful. Nevis is not the kind of place where you build white houses." And since the clients were vehemently against pastels, bold, saturated colors were the way to go.

The architects' inspiration came from far away—the pigmented houses of Africa, Brazil, and Argentina—and nearby. Nevis itself is filled with color, from the bright hats worn by churchgoing women to the rich plantings of ginger blossoms, heliconias, and orchids that grow wild over the island, which is home to 9,500 people as well as a healthy population of monkeys, wild donkeys, and the occasional movie star ensconced at the Four Seasons.

The three houses all roughly face southeast, with views of azure waters where the Atlantic Ocean and Caribbean Sea converge.

The Parish Ground residence, the largest of the three, has the most complex plan. From a parking lot at the end of the access road, guests go up a staircase and into a grassy courtyard defined by yellow walls. An inviting daybed hangs from the roof of a porch overlooking the court. Around the corner is a double-height open-air stair hall with a doorway that leads to the kitchen, dining terrace, and another courtyard; stairs that lead up to the master suite; and steps that go down to a landscaped courtyard with a lotus pond that Morello calls "the secret garden," and a living-room pavilion beyond. Beneath the living room is a secluded guest suite reached from the courtyard, flanking a spectacular cobalt-blue swimming pool with an infinity edge that blurs into a view of the open sea. The outside of the house is a deep blue; each of the interior spaces is a different color. The kitchen is bright green, the powder room magenta, the stair hall citrus yellow, and the living room red-orange. Only the master suite is neutral, with warm hues coming from the grays of concrete floors and walls, and deep reddish browns of wooden louver doors and wood-paneled ceilings. Behind the house is a freestanding service building finished in turquoise-tinted concrete.

The Liburds estate, located uphill from Parish Ground, is considerably smaller. Unlike its neighbor, Liburds is inwardly focused. The U-shaped house wraps around a small outdoor courtyard densely planted with palms and banana trees. A staircase leads up to an open-air porch exposed to the sea, which in turn opens onto a dining room and kitchen on one side, and a living room on the other. Downstairs are two bedrooms, an open terrace, and space for a large cistern. One wing of the U-shaped house is a light-red color, the other a deep blue. The bright green living room has louvered wood windows on two sides and a peaked wood-paneled ceiling.

The most colorful of the three houses is the Gingerland residence, located higher uphill than the other two houses. It's also the smallest and the most abstract of the three homes, with bolder lines and simpler surfaces. The exterior includes a yellow wing, but the core of the house is blue, with a deep-red wall marking the entry up a flight of steps—a veritable

Parish Ground House

Ground floor plan

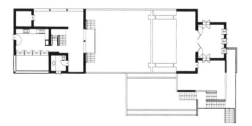

Second floor plan

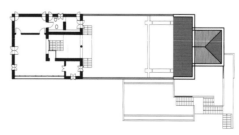

The home is filled with cool, loft-like spaces finished in pigmented concrete. **Right:** An infinity-edge pool framed in a colorful concrete wall overlooks the green hills and blue Caribbean waters off the coast of Nevis.

Mondrian canvas. The ground floor contains the living room and an open-air dining space. Upstairs, crowned by a magnificent wood-paneled ceiling, the master bedroom fills the the center of the house; louvered doors open onto a sunny terrace. In the works is a planned addition, with studio and expanded terrace and patio space.

All three houses were built using poured-in-place concrete and concrete block. Given the scarcity of building materials on Nevis, as well as the island's active seismic zone, it's a perfect construction system. The homes' characteristic color schemes were created using a lime-based pigment rubbed onto the finished concrete surfaces, not the typical paint or concrete dye.

Liburds Estate House

Ground floor plan **Second floor plan**

Tropical vegetation grows
wild over the concrete
structures, which
connect to the outdoors
with louvered doors and
windows and plenty of
outdoor living spaces.
The airy, minimalist
living room (above right)
features bright green
walls and a towering
pitched ceiling covered
in slats of wood.
Left: A lush courtyard
greets visitors to the
Liburds Estate house.

With such color saturation in their design, and so much natural color surrounding it, MORSA wisely kept the interiors simple, almost Spartan. The most exuberant moments are Gingerland House's Memphis-style black-and-white checkerboard wall in the living room, and bands of orange and yellow pigment in the master suite. The rest of the spaces are cool and calm, animated by the wall colors, as well as the bright sunlight and cooling trade winds.

Although no glass or screens cover any of the doors and windows, the constant breeze seems to keep the mosquitoes at bay. But because there are termites, all of the wood in the three houses, including door and window frames, cabinets, and paneling, is ipé, a tropical hardwood too dense for termites' tastes.

Monkeys are another story. Savoie and Morello report that the houses' bold colors have attracted local monkeys in droves—a ringing endorsement about just how fitting these colorful houses are for this tropical island.

Gingerland House

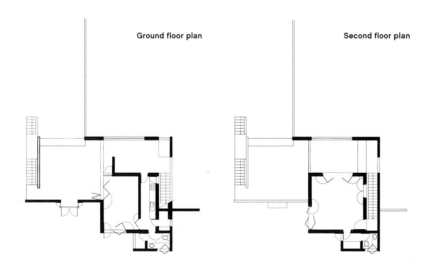

Ground floor plan   Second floor plan

Spacious outdoor decks
framing views of the
Caribbean with colorful
walls have echoes of the
work of Mexican
modernist Luis Barragán.
Left: Louvered wood
doors and shutters warm
up the spare, minimalist
volumes. The master
bedroom features a
towering ceiling finished
in rich wood and bands
of color that lend an
African air.

Weiss Residence
Cabo San Lucas Mexico

Just below the Tropic of Cancer at the tip of Baja California is the southernmost house on the Mexican peninsula: the Weiss residence, designed by New York architect Steven Harris. The house is a sprawling 9,000-square-foot ensemble of open and enclosed living spaces and fully furnished outdoor rooms nestled among boulders and desert gardens, towering 250 feet above the deep blue waters of the Pacific Ocean.

Working with landscape designer Margie Ruddick and interior designer Lucien Rees-Roberts, Harris created a luxurious getaway that fit his clients' desire for a home in a "martini modern" style. There's more than a passing resemblance to the slick, mid-century modern houses of the Hollywood Hills and Rat Pack–era Palm Springs: clean lines, sleek lounge-flavored furniture, and a cool color palette. But Harris also took into account the dramatic, arid landscape of Baja California, as well as the local tradition of reinforced concrete construction. Though it has a strong personality, the house easily blends into the stark colors and rugged forms of its surroundings.

Harris wove the desert landscape into the architecture in an open promenade of indoor and outdoor spaces. The entrance leads down to the site from street level. An entry path winds down from a parking lot along a solid rock staircase and a ramp that leads to a small foyer. The foyer opens onto an arid courtyard filled with exotic desert plants and rock formations. Harris designed three separate spaces around the courtyard, deferring to the natural topography. He oriented different rooms to different views, while securing privacy from neighboring houses.

Along the southern edge of the court is an L-shaped wing containing the master suite, media room, and gym. On the opposite side are an open-air dining room, a glass-enclosed living room, and kitchen. Toward the ocean is one of the home's most inventive, truly tropical spaces: an open-air living room that seems to hover above the boulders. This isn't just an outdoor deck; Harris treated it as a fully furnished room that happens to have no walls. (There is one partial wall on which art is hung.) The space is completely open to the elements, without so much as a sliding-glass door between the corner columns and flat concrete-slab roof.

None of the three guestrooms are visible from the main level—they're tucked beneath the ground floor, bermed into the steep hill as it drops to the sea. One guestroom is located beneath the main living room; the others are two levels below the outdoor living room. Nestled against a rock outcropping at the corner of the site is a lap pool facing the sea. Guest quarters, pool deck, and study are reached by stone steps leading down from the courtyard.

Harris anchored the house by burrowing into the hillside, creating sheltered rooms that contrast with the daring cantilevered spaces enclosed in glass along the ocean side. The media and exercise rooms have walls of exposed rock illuminated by narrow strip skylights. Embedded into their east-facing walls is a grid of glass rods that cast circles of light with the morning sun.

The wall of glass rods and the light-washed stone walls are just two of the sexy, sophisticated plays of tropical sunlight Harris introduced into the house. Indoors and out, powerful

Just one-story high at street level, the Weiss house extends vertically down a steep cliff to open up multiple floors to views of the Pacific Ocean.
Following pages: The house is composed of three freestanding pavilions, built of concrete, glass, and native Mexican stone, that are grouped around a central courtyard and oriented to the ocean view.

sunlight is tempered with roof overhangs. Harris also manipulates it to subtle effect with hidden skylights, slender clerestories, water runnels, and reflecting pools. Where he needed glass to properly define a space, high-strength laminated glazing with custom stainless-steel anchors brace against hurricane winds.

The Weiss house is as sleek and stylish as any sophisticated urban suite, yet deeply rooted in its tropical setting. Harris custom-tailored its "martini modern" style to the rustic cliffside, optimizing sunlight, views, and open-air living to create a civilized tropical retreat.

Strong and subtle plays of daylight wash across the home's smooth and textured surfaces. **Following pages:** Many of the living spaces, including the dining room (top left) and an informal sitting area (bottom left) are completely open to the elements, while the formal living room is sheltered by walls of hurricane-resistant floor-to-ceiling glass (top right). A bedroom is buried in the rocky hillside (bottom right).

Site plan

Entry-level floor plan

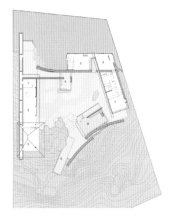

Section through site

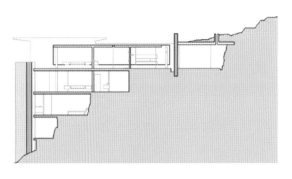

Gamma-Issa Residence

São Paulo Brazil

São Paulo architect Márcio Kogan often collaborates with longtime friend Isay Weinfeld. Their complementary architectural styles are evident in a house Kogan designed in São Paulo's elegant Alto de Pinheiros district. Whereas Weinfeld's houses temper hard-edged modernism with rich woods and indigenous stone, Kogan's design for a couple that works in advertising pushes pure minimalism to the extreme.

Kogan's clients wanted a home inspired by an eclectic mix of influences, from 1960s furniture and electronic music to *Visionaire* magazine and Jacques Tati's surrealist film *Mon Oncle*. They also wanted an enormous double-height living room, a 100-foot-long swimming pool, a comfortable office and studio, and, quite specifically, an orange table for informal lunches.

Kogan obliged by designing a 7,500-square-foot house with a single volume which fulfills all of its functions: a simple white box amid the chaos of the city, which Kogan calls "the wold's ugliest, but overflowing with energy, vibrant like no other, loved and hated." A sleek wooden fence screens out the tropical metropolis; a white sliding door leads into a clean foyer, which opens into the dramatic double-height living room. The 20-foot-high room is a crisp white volume with two sets of stacked, floor-to-ceiling bookshelves placed symmetrically at either end. The top bookshelves are placed along the mezzanine, which leads to the bedrooms.

One set of shelves defines the living area, with stark modernist furniture, including a classic Achille Castiglioni arc lamp and Eero Aarnio's retro-futurist ball chair. The other set is the backdrop to the dining area, centered on an Eero Saarinen table with Jasper Morrison's Glo-Bal lights floating above. Kogan made one of the walls a series of towering floor-to-ceiling glass doors that open the room completely to an enclosed garden. The courtyard creates a thick green carpet that sets off the pure white house.

The ground floor also contains a TV room and spacious work studio with sliding-glass doors that open onto a narrow gravel-covered courtyard on the east side of the house. Along the north side is the kitchen—with the orange dining counter—overlooking another narrow walled garden. Upstairs, behind the bookshelves along the stair landing is a pair of bedrooms with separate baths. The luxurious master suite takes up the rest of the second floor. A private terrace extends through the length of the suite.

Kogan kept the palette simple and minimalist: whitewashed walls, Brazilian cumarú wood floors, and swaths of marble and stainless steel in the bathrooms and kitchen. Instead of Brazilian-designed furniture, he opted largely for sleek contemporary and classic modern pieces by European designers like Bertoia and Saarinen.

Amid the urban bustle of São Paulo, the integrated indoor-outdoor spaces and sunlit gardens and courtyards of Kogan's house make it an extraordinary tropical home. He took advantage of the sun's brightness at this latitude to create smooth, abstract white surfaces that reflect the strong light in an even wash. In this tropical setting, minimalism and high-modern furnishings take on a whole new flavor.

Day and night, the 20-foot-tall living-dining room is a spectacular space with a wall of sliding glass doors that open the room to the outdoors.
Following pages: The front door slides open to reveal a small, whitewashed foyer and the dramatic living-dining room beyond, filled with classic modernist furnishings.

Kogan created a soothing house amid São Paulo's urban bustle with indoor-outdoor spaces and sunlit courtyards and gardens. He maximized the brightness of the tropical sun with smooth, white surfaces that reflect the strong sunlight in an even wash.

Above left: The luminous all-white master bath features a deep marble tub.
Above right: A brightly colored dining counter in the kitchen overlooks a walled-in garden.
Right: The master bedroom is another pale glowing space with windows overlooking the backyard garden.

Ground floor plan

Second floor plan

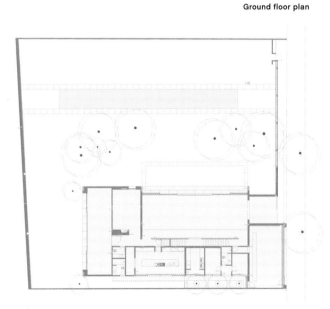

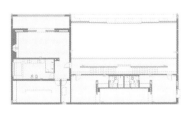

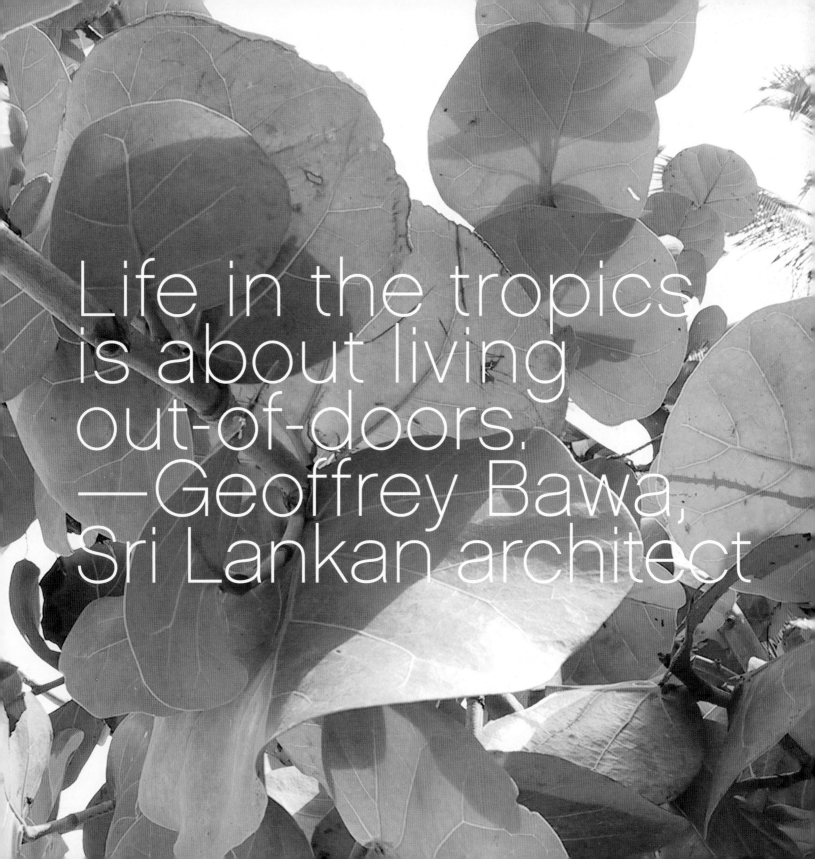

Life in the tropics
is about living
out-of-doors.
—Geoffrey Bawa,
Sri Lankan architect

Luis Guillermo Pons, design architect

Figueroa Residence

Miami Beach Florida U.S.A.

Longitudinal section

Transverse section

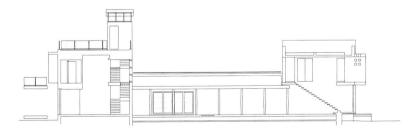

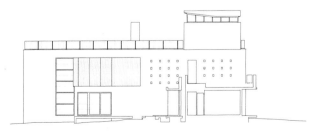

Ground floor plan

Second floor plan

Cool, elegant travertine walls enclosing a double-height entry hall separate the dining room (top right) from the spacious living room (top left). **Right:** A wall of floor-to-ceiling windows overlooking the bay extends from the dining room towards the living room, both finished in teak floors.

John Hix, Architect

Casa Triangular

Vieques
Puerto
Rico

Canadian-based architect John Hix and his wife, Neeva Gayle, spent many years vacationing on Vieques. Eventually they bought property on the south coast of Vieques—a rambling hillside with views of the lush hills, undeveloped beaches, and Caribbean waters—and began building a residential compound located near the top of the hill. Hix's initial plans for his home and studio looked to the island's modest wood houses with galvanized metal roofs for inspiration. After Hurricane Hugo devastated Vieques and neighboring islands, stripping vegetation bare and destroying fragile wood-framed homes, Hix decided instead to build in concrete.

A concrete house made sense on many fronts. It could withstand hurricanes, brush fires, and the occasional Caribbean earthquakes. It would also be a low-maintenance alternative, free from the rotting and warping of wood in the tropical humidity, and would allow the architect to use local craftsmen skilled in concrete building. Extensive plans for concrete surfaces—floors, walls, ceilings, even countertops and dining tables honed to a smooth, reflective finish—gave Vieques's craftsmen a chance to show off their skills.

Hix's house may be solid as a bunker, but it is also completely open to the outdoors. In fact, there isn't a pane of glass or an insect screen in the many windows and doors that open in every direction, facing views of grassy hills and turquoise waters. Hix oriented the structure to prevailing trade winds from the southeast and placed windows and doors to encourage cross-ventilation, so there's a constant breeze flowing through the house and no need for air conditioning. Ceiling fans boost air circulation when the trade winds slow or when it's especially warm, but most of the time natural breezes are enough. On a winter night, it can get downright chilly with the windows open. The airflow keeps down the insect population, but mosquito netting over the beds is still necessary.

In the plan, the four-level house is a triangle nestled into the south-facing hillside. The ground level space, originally a garage, is now Hix's architecture studio. There is still a small kitchen and an open-air shower tucked into one of the points of the triangular footprint. The main level, where the couple spends a good part of the year, is an open, loft-like space which encompasses a kitchen with built-in concrete dining table, a bathroom with open-air shower, a workspace, and a sleeping area. There's also a spacious, open living area with a curved panoramic view of the Caribbean, and a dining terrace just outside the kitchen with a large metal table perfect for shady breakfasts al fresco. The third level has another guest suite with two outdoor terraces (one with a framed view of the neighboring hillside) and separate kitchen. From here, an oddly proportioned stair leads up to a roof deck with a cactus garden, where the couple envisioned guests congregating for cocktails at sunset. It's also a perfect spot for stargazing on a moonless night.

The furnishings throughout the house are simple, almost Spartan. Hix designed a series of painted wood tables, chaise lounges, and arm chairs inspired by Gerrit Rietveld's de Stijl furniture. Otherwise, there isn't much furniture, since the concrete tables, counters, and desks are all built-in. Hix left the exterior concrete facade to weather naturally to minimize maintenance, but painted interior walls in palettes ranging from pale blues to yellows and terra-cotta.

Hix's architecture has elements of the polychrome Mexican modernism of Luis Barragán, and of Louis Kahn, with whom he studied at the University of Pennsylvania in the 1960s.

Casa Triangular is indeed a triangle in both plan and elevation. Each level of the weathered concrete house includes a self-contained guest apartment with large openings framing views of the green hills and blue Caribbean.

It also boasts varying shades of "greenness" that earned Hix an Environmental Quality Award from the U.S. Environmental Protection Agency: from the dense vegetation he let creep over the exteriors, to its semi-self-sufficient energy sources (solar panels that power water heaters, lights, and ceiling fans), to irrigation of the tropical landscape with gray-water runoff from showers and sinks. Beyond that, there's closeness with nature in the sun and moon glimpsed through open showers and views at every turn.

Hix moved his architecture studio to the bottom unit and now rents out the top unit as part of a guest house that includes two larger concrete structures, each with five loft-like studio apartments, a pool with changing rooms, yoga studio, and lobby. These recent additions make Hix's brand of tropical minimalism accessible to adventurous, design-minded travelers.

Roof deck plan

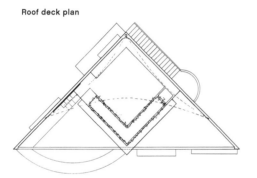

Third floor plan

Second floor plan

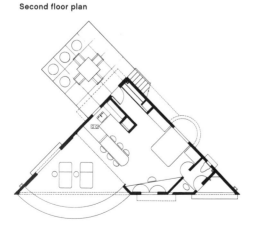

Ground floor plan

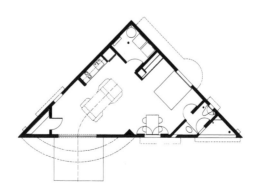

Large rectangular cutouts in the west façade are places to sit and contemplate the view. Next to the front door of the ground floor suite is an outdoor dining terrace with a handy access window to the kitchen.
Following pages:
Casa Triangular's concrete floors, walls, ceilings, and built-in desktops and counters create a minimalist, lofty atmosphere. Rustic wood shutters are the primary enclosures.

Victoria Park House

Singapore

The lush, orderly tropical island-nation of Singapore lies just eighty-five miles north of the equator, which means that the sun shines overhead all year long, with average high temperatures that rarely go below upper 80s (F). Singapore is also incredibly rainy and humid, with variations in rainfall marking the only real distinction between seasons. Throughout the year it rains in tropical fashion—potent downpours followed by sun—but during monsoon season, from November through January, the rain can be torrential, lasting for days on end. Such climate conditions force architects in Singapore to focus on keeping out the rain and the sun, using natural ventilation to offer some relief from the oppressive heat and humidity or else give in to sealed air-conditioned interiors.

Soo Chan of SCD Architects designs homes tailored to Singapore's climate by integrating landscape and water, blurring indoors and outdoors. Chan likes to make homes of "tranquility and calmness qualified by space, light, and structural order." He designed a house in suburban Victoria Park that's sophisticated yet open and breezy, an oasis of calm in the middle of suburbia.

Commissioned for a middle-aged couple whose children are studying abroad, Victoria Park is a modern, tropical take on the traditional courtyard house. Chan organized the home around a swimming pool that extends up to the edges of the structure and seems to flow inside.

The house sits on a hillside sloping roughly fifteen feet from front to back. Guests arriving by car pull into a driveway that slips beneath the house and walk up a flight of stairs that leads up to an outdoor foyer. To the right of the entry is the living area. Straight ahead is a long corridor—the spine on the ground floor that links the kitchen, dining room, guestroom, and maid's room with private second-floor quarters—with glass doors overlooking the pool. Upstairs are three bedrooms and a master suite, all overlooking the pool court.

Despite its location in a densely populated suburb on a relatively tight lot, the most inviting aspect of the house is its openness to the outdoors. Along the main-floor hallway, for instance, French doors open onto the pool to draw in cooling breezes. Sliding-glass doors define three sides of the living room, and can be opened completely to create a semi-outdoor space, framed by the pool and coconut palms that screen out the neighbors. Deep overhanging roofs shade the interiors from a blazing equatorial sun and protect them from the heavy rains. They also create layers of space that mark a gentle transition from the hot, tropical outdoors to the cool, calming indoors.

Large sliding glass doors wrap the living room, which is shaded by deep roof overhangs. An L-shaped pool flows right up to edge of the house.

Section through living room

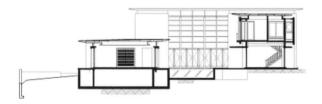

Section through foyer

Section through bedroom wing

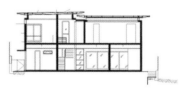

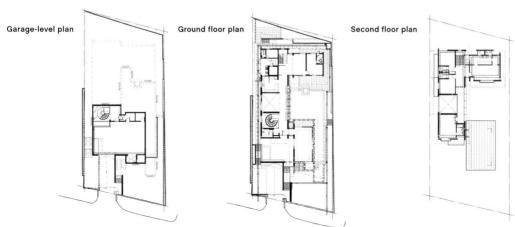

Garage-level plan

Ground floor plan

Second floor plan

With the sliding glass doors thrown open, the living room (above right and the following page) becomes an open-air space along the water's edge, cooled by breezes flowing across the pool.
Following pages: The deep eaves and solid walls of the bedroom wing (right) shade the interiors from the strong equatorial sun.

Architecture is the masterly, correct and magnificent play of masses brought together in light.
—Le Corbusier

Jayawardene House
Mirissa
Sri Lanka

Sri Lanka's Geoffrey Bawa is one of the most celebrated modern architects in Southeast Asia. In a prolific career spanning more than forty years, Bawa has made his mark on the former British colony of Ceylon with stellar houses, university buildings, luxurious beachfront resorts, and the new Sri Lankan parliament outside the capital, Colombo. His buildings reveal an earthy minimalist style and a deep sensitivity to the tropical climate and landscape of his native country. Like the culture of Sri Lanka, Bawa's designs draw from a mix of influences, from European modernism to traditional Indian and Ceylonese architecture.

The Jayawardene house is the last Bawa designed before being paralyzed by a stroke in 1998, at the age of seventy-nine. Commissioned as a weekend retreat by the grandson of a former Sri Lankan president, the house is more a pleasure pavilion than a proper home. Circled by thickets of towering coconut palms and stately old pines overlooking the beaches of Weligama Bay, the structure follows the footprint of a vacation house enjoyed by former President Jayawardene's family, which was destroyed by fire in the late 1980s. Jayawardene's grandson bought the property and commissioned Bawa to capture the spirit of this seaside spot, not to re-create the architecture of his family's vanished retreat. The sprawling, industrial-looking structure sits high above the Indian Ocean along the cliffs of Mirissa, an historic fishing village in the southeast corner of Sri Lanka.

An enormous living and dining area covers the ground floor of the 4,000-square-foot home, resembling an airplane hangar open to the sea. Sheltering the vast open space with raw concrete floors is a thin roof of galvanized steel and aluminum supported on a grid of slender reinforced-concrete columns. Concrete steps at the back of the long rectangular space lead to a Spartan al fresco sitting room that doubles as a sleeping area for overnight guests. Though it seems almost desolate when empty, the space comes alive during frequent dinner parties thrown by the client. Lively dinners take place around a 25-foot-long built-in dining table resting on the remnants of two old generators. Downstairs is a more private world, with a study, small pantry, two bedrooms, and bathrooms partially buried into the hillside. The idea behind putting these spaces downstairs was twofold: to keep uninterrupted views on the main floor, and to create calm, secure shelter where the family could seek refuge during Sri Lanka's torrential monsoons.

According to Channa Daswatte, one of Bawa's collaborators on the project, this is "the quintessential tropical house" because it provides shelter from the sun and rain and allows cool breezes to flow through the house unimpeded: "It follows the long tradition of open pavilions that are the essence of building in this part of the world." In fact, Daswatte calls this minimalist domain a modern version of "ambalama," a roadside resting place in Sri Lanka.

The pavilionlike weekend house is a spare, modern version of a Sri Lankan roadside resting place. An open-air living and sleeping area sits above lower-level bedrooms. **Following pages:** A glass-enclosed staircase leads down to the bedroom level.

This is "the quintessential tropical house" because it provides shelter from the sun and rain and allows cooling breezes to flow through the house unimpeded.

Site plan

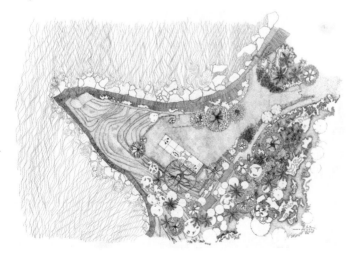

The remnants of a pair of electrical generators form the base of a built-in industrial dining table that is the centerpiece of large weekend dinner parties.

Sandbank House

St. Thomas
U.S. Virgin
Islands

Isay Weinfeld, architect

Bitter
Residence
Tijucopava
Brazil

While the Cariocas of Rio de Janeiro have the world-famous beaches of Copacabana and Ipanema at their doorstep, the Paulistas of bustling São Paulo must hop in their cars and brave the city's choking traffic to get to the sea. But unlike Rio's jam-packed beaches, the coastline just ninety minutes south of São Paulo is serene. One popular quiet spot for week-end escapes from São Paulo is the town of Tijucopava, where architect Isay Weinfeld designed a 6,500-square-foot beachfront getaway for the Bitter family, owners of a textile company that produces fabric for many of Brazil's top fashion designers.

From the street, the home is a cool, minimalist composition of white volumes, with a tower and parking pad sheltered by a long concrete slab. Weinfeld enjoys surprising his visitors: A hidden doorway from the parking area leads to an outdoor arcade bordering a palm-studded lawn. The interior wall of the arcade is covered in a rough patchwork of white Portuguese mosaics, akin to the tiles found in Roberto Burle Marx's famous wave-patterned sidewalks along Ipanema and Copacabana. The walkway is finished in rich ipé wood. At the end of the open-air hall, a soaring 16-foot-tall room with towering glass doors opens onto a pool deck and a stunning view of the sea. These doors and another set looking back on the entry lawn pivot open to let the ocean breeze flow right through the light-drenched interior.

The dramatic living-dining room is the first space you encounter, but is really the back end of a long, narrow floor plan that extends from the ocean to the road. Tucked behind a stair-case without railings is the kitchen, with granite floors and Formica walls, which leads back to a service wing with a spare bedroom, laundry facilities, storage, and staff quarters.

An upstairs balcony with an informal fitness room overlooks the living-dining area. Behind the balcony is a hallway that leads to the bedrooms. There's no shortage of space for overnight guests: Weinfeld designed six bedrooms on this level, like a deck of spacious cabins in a glamorous cruise ship. Each has its own private bathroom with a round skylight and small sitting area. The bedroom at the far end of the hall is the largest, with a walk-in closet that leads to a spacious bathroom. All the bedroom windows, shaded by aluminum screens, overlook the entry garden. Another flight of stairs off the mezzanine-level gym leads to the master suite, which boasts a large window overlooking the ocean. Above it is a private roof deck shaded by a canvas sail—a stylish crow's nest with sweeping views of the coastline.

Weinfeld designed the house in a simple palette of rustic Portuguese mosaics, ipé wood floors and decks, and polished surfaces. The living-dining room has a white marble floor which reflects daylight flooding in through the wall of glass doors; the hallways and balcony feature native Brazilian Perobinha do Campo wood; the bedrooms and bathrooms are finished in all-white ceramic and glass mosaic tiles.

This is a beach house designed for entertaining lots of guests in a simple, elegant style. The living-dining room is dramatic, but it's really a giant porch from which to sit and eat while watching the waves break. Of course, it's an extremely refined house, not a dress-down beach shack. What makes it sophisticated is immaterial: Weinfeld's use of space and light. The house is tropical in its lightness of touch, and modern in its evanescent quality, which lets the sun and surf take center stage.

The home's whitewashed street façade (top) is solid, while its beachfront elevation opens to the elements with towering glass doors.

Third floor plan

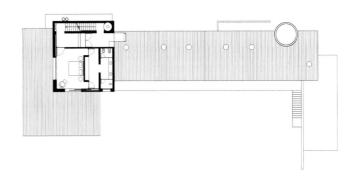

Second floor plan

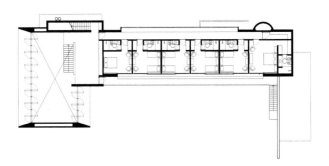

A wall of 16-foot-tall glass doors pivots open to transform the airy, elegant living-dining room into a giant open-air porch with views of the sea.
Following pages: A dramatic handrail-free staircase leads from the dining area, with a phalanx of Eames chairs, up to the bedroom level.
Overleaf: The outdoor corridor leading from the street to the main entrance is lined with a Portuguese mosaic wall. The home's crowning glory is a rooftop deck covered with a canvas sail and sweeping views of the Brazilian coastline.

Ground floor plan

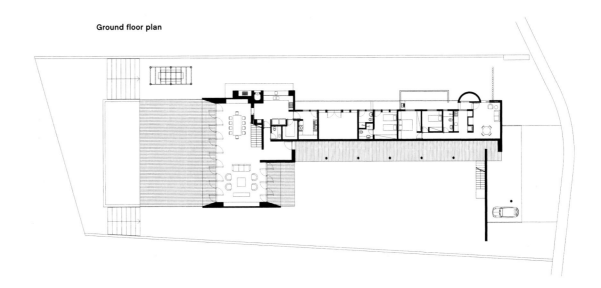

There is no reason for architecture dictated by the land, the topography, and the climate and site conditions

not to be good
architecture.
In that way it's
possible to create
architecture
of the tropics.
—Walter James
Alcock, Venezuelan
architect

Innovarchi, architect

Gold Coast House
Reedy Creek
Australia

The Gold Coast is Australia's answer to South Florida: strips of glittering high-rise hotels and condominiums straddle the subtropical Pacific beaches of northern New South Wales and southern Queensland. There's even a town called Miami and resorts named Surfer's Paradise and Palm Beach. And like Florida, the Gold Coast is hot, humid, and rainy in summer, often with temperatures above 40° C (104° F). As you move inland, the crowded beaches and twinkling oceanfront towers give way to the lush woodlands, rain forests, and brush-covered hills of the so-called Hinterlands. (The local visitors' bureau touts the region as "the green behind the Gold.") On a hillside near the tourist hamlet of Mudgereeba just six kilometers from the coast, Sydney architects Stephanie Smith and Ken McBryde of Innovarchi designed a 5,400-square-foot vacation house that opens itself up to the warm weather and panoramic views of the ocean and forested hillside.

McBryde and Smith say they didn't want to create a cute cottage or beachfront bungalow; they wanted a modern glass box, as open to the outdoors as possible—"a fishbowl with somewhere to get dressed." Their clients, dance instructor Prudence Bowen and her husband Richard Lennox, are not avid beachgoers, but still enjoy the warm weather and easygoing resort lifestyle. According to McBryde, Bowen's late father was an architect who instilled in her a "passion for hard-core modern." Smith and McBryde added their own affinity for sleek, hard-edged materials: the two are alumni of master architect Renzo Piano's office, having collaborated with Piano on large-scale projects like the Kansai airport in Osaka, Japan.

Bowen's house is really two buildings: A pair of bi-level pavilions separated by a deck above the parking pad, with exterior staircases that lead to two separate living quarters—one for Bowen and Lennox, the other for Juliette, Bowen's elderly mother. The base of the couple's wing contains an art gallery and ballet studio; the ground floor of the mother's wing contains a guestroom, artist's studio, and Lennox's office. Upstairs, both wings contain open living, dining, and bedroom spaces, plus a kitchen and bath, all sheathed in floor-to-ceiling glass. Bowen, an accomplished dance instructor in Australia, often hosts aspiring young ballerinas for two-week stints. They take up residence in the guest suite, practice in the studio, and give performances on the deck between the two glass compartments.

Essentially, the two wings are spacious lofts wrapped in detailed crystalline skins and set atop black concrete-block bases. There is one concession to a traditional Australian space: a long, outdoor verandah adjoining the living areas. Sliding-glass doors and continuous concrete floors extend the verandah indoors.

The house's casual interiors have the openness and sophisticated polish of urban lofts, but are perfectly suited to the casual lifestyle of a summer beach house. Glass facades afford panoramic views of the ocean and the Hinterlands, drawing them in as backdrops. The combination of glass louver windows, sliding panes, and pivoting doors also open up interior rooms to the outdoors, keeping fresh air circulating naturally. Glass doors in the bathroom open to create the feeling of an outdoor shower or bath. Even in this tropical fishbowl, privacy can be had by drawing moveable wooden screen to shield the bathrooms.

Open floor plans help air ventilation by keeping operable windows close together. Originally from temperate Sydney, Bowen balked initially at the idea of louver windows, but now loves them and would be happy to have more, according to McBryde. Deep roof overhangs and

The home's transparent living spaces, focused on distant views of the Pacific Ocean, are glass-enclosed pavilions atop solid concrete bases.

motorized blinds bring shade and keep the interiors from becoming sweltering green-houses in the summer. Concrete floor slabs and concrete-block walls also play a part in keeping the house cool. They provide thermal mass: they store the coolness of the evening air and radiate it back during the daytime, and do the opposite at night with the stored heat of the day. This is a big improvement on the traditional tropical Queensland house in Australia, built of lightweight wood but without thermal mass. "They're beautiful, but they heat up with the day. So you freeze in winter and in summer all you can do is hope for a breeze for some relief," says McBryde. Not so in Innovarchi's polished hideaway in the Hinterlands.

Deep roof overhangs shield the second-floor glass facades from the strong sun; downstairs are studio and gallery spaces.
Following pages: The open, loft-like living quarters spill out seamlessly onto modern versions of traditional Australian verandahs.

Section

Ground floor plan

Second floor plan

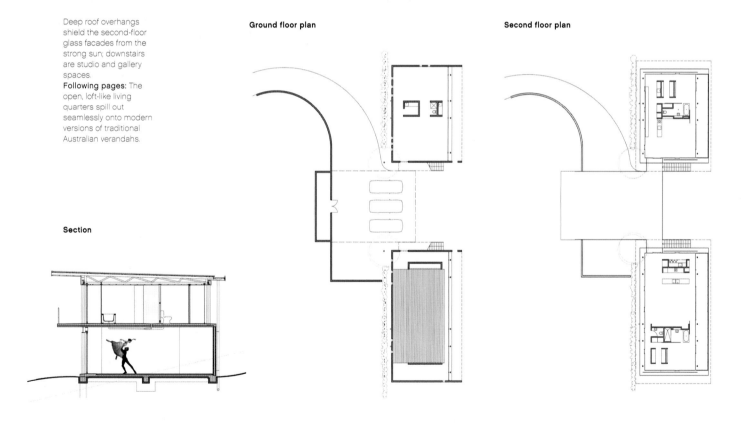

Walter James Alcock, original architect
Keenen/Riley, interior renovation architect

La
Ribereña
Caracas
Venezuela

In forty-four years of practice, Venezuelan architect Walter James Alcock has designed dozens of banks, hotels, housing projects, and schools as expressive, experimental structures of concrete and brick. Alcock's houses are some of his most daring and luxurious projects. Many of them enjoy spectacular settings in the hills of Caracas; all of them share a deep understanding and appreciation of the Caribbean climate, with outdoor rooms, open-air promenades, and lush gardens that blend architecture and landscape.

In 1976, Alcock designed a house called La Ribereña, at the foot of El Avila Mountain in Caracas. More than three decades later, New York architects Keenen/Riley did a light renovation of the house—architect John Keenen calls it a "minimal intervention"—and replaced all of its furnishings. The only functional change the architects made to Alcock's original plan was to turn an underused office into extra living space.

Alcock built the house entirely in brick and concrete, not the most obvious choice of materials for the tropics. But despite associations with buildings in colder climates, along with references to the work of Finnish architect Alvar Aalto, La Ribereña is extremely tropical: It unfolds as a series of interconnected rooms, many of which open to gardens, linked by open-air hallways filled with lush tropical plantings. The main garden designed by Brazilian modernist landscaper Roberto Burle Marx is one of the highlights, boasting a waterfall and angular pool with an Alexander Calder sculpture.

From the street, the house gives the impression of being a solid brick wall. At the center of the entry wall is a cube, rotated at forty-five degrees, marking the entrance. The angled foyer leads to an open arcade ending in a skylit indoor garden and an open-air living and dining room, which overlooks the Burle Marx garden and pool.

According to Keenen, the clients spend less time in the enclosed areas of the house. They prefer to live in the open spaces, eating dinner on an outdoor terrace or relaxing in the big family room with a view of the main garden.

Throughout the home, Keenen/Riley selected a mix of old and new furnishings. "The house allowed for a certain eclecticism," says Keenen. The house has a modern yet timeless feel, which inspired the use of contemporary furniture, mid-century pieces, and a smattering of antiques from the home's previous owners. There are rattan chairs, woven leather ottomans, sleek contemporary Italian sofas and chairs, and showpieces by classic mid-century modernists like Gio Ponti, Arne Jacobsen, Franco Albini, and Ico Parisi. The architects used a lot of warm wood furniture, which they thought would harmonize with and soften the surrounding brick, terrazzo, and concrete surfaces.

The architecture, though minimalist, offers strong sensory experiences. Masonry and terrazzo cast the interiors in a cool and quiet—almost monastic—mood. Ornamental metal gates and grilles create bold, patterned shadows across the floors. The open architecture brings the outdoors within: the sounds of the water, the scent of the gardens, warm breezes. In some aspects, Alcock's design is an unusual choice for the tropics; but La Ribereña couldn't be more suited to its setting. The house is sophisticated, full of atmosphere, and a timeless example of tropical modern style.

Lush tropical plantings flank the terrazzo-paved corridor linking the foyer and the living room.

Isometric view

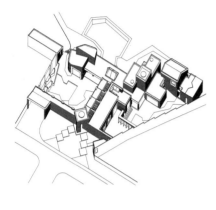

Cut-away isometric view

Floor plan

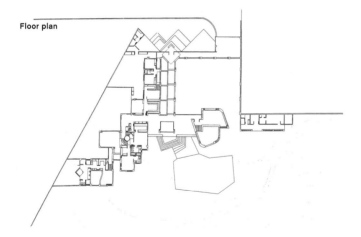

Section through main corridor

Beyond a floor-to-ceiling art piece installed on a dining room wall is an open-air terrace enclosed by patterned metal grilles.
Following pages: Sheltered beneath the exposed concrete ribs supporting an angular roof is a formal indoor living room (left) and master bedroom (right).
Overleaf: Tropical sunlight washes a sculptural staircase (left). The Burle Marx–designed garden contains contains a sculpture by Alexander Calder (right).

Acknowledgements

So many people around the world offered insights, ideas, support, and inspiration in putting this book together. I'd like to thank all the architects whose work fills these pages, especially Isay Weinfeld for his gentle nature and intense passion for design; his work was a major inspiration behind this entire project. Thank you also to the many photographers who contributed images, especially Erica Stoller at ESTO, Tuca Reinés, Luis Gordoa, Christian Richters, Michael Moran, Undine Pröhl, and Åke E:son Lindman. And certainly not least, my deepest thanks to the inspired clients who commissioned these spectacular homes.

Thank you to Charles Miers and Steve Case at Rizzoli/Universe for pushing this project through swiftly, and to Claudia Brandenburg for yet another fruitful and entertaining graphic collaboration.

Thanks also to Terence Riley at the Museum of Modern Art for his valuable suggestions and his continued support of modernist architecture in Latin America, and to John Keenen, the other half of Keenen/Riley, for his insights and contributions to modernism in the tropics.

My appreciation to all of the following who made this book a truly global collaboration.

In New York: Arlene Hirst at *Metropolitan Home;* Robert Ivy, Sara Hart, and Jim Russell at *Architectural Record;* Gordon Kipping; Gabriella di Ferrari; Antonio Zaninovic; Bree Jeppson and Markus Dochantschi; Nina Rappaport; Jim Franco; Carlos Brillembourg; Rosalie Genevro at the Architectural League of New York; Sergio Guardia; Giovanni Bianco; Jan Greben; Andrea Schwan; Aric Chen; David Rockwell; Eve Kahn; Julia Joern; Deborah Berke; Belmont Freeman; Alexandra Brez

In Miami: Magaly Acosta; Jennifer Rubell; Laura Sheridan; Troy Campbell; the Figueroa family

In Europe: Laura Houseley; William Wareing; Judy Dobias; Tyler Brûlé

In Puerto Rico: José Toro; Gonzalo Ferrer; Jean-Pierre Santoni; Glorimar Ortiz; Nataniel Fúster; Margarita Fullana; Roberto Gonzalez; Luis Fernando Rodriguez; Annie Velez; John and Neeva Gayle Hix; Ricardo Quesada and Ray Freeman; Baby Llenza; Ricardo, Monica, and Gabu Betancourt

In Australia: Davina Jackson; Brit Andresen; Alex Popov; Alec Tzannes; Kerry and Lindsay Clare

In Mexico: Enrique Norten; Felipe Leal; Miquel Adriá

In Brazil: Flavia de Faria; Zeca Sa Ferreira; Arthur de Mattos Casas; Carolina Maluhy; the Instituto Bardi; Nelson Kon

Elsewhere: Marialidia Marcotulli; Fabio Marcotulli; Rick Joy; Odile Henault; Brigitte Shim; Raveevarn Choksombatchai; Hiranti Welandawe; Lisa Findley; Brian Bullen at COCOA/The Caribbean Office of Cooperative Architecture; Ivonne Valencia and José Maria Rodriguez; Ernesto Bedmar; Dung Ngo; Claudia Perrino; Jim Sonzero

Credits

Introduction

p. 13 Ezra Stoller/ESTO, pp. 14-15 Åke E:son Lindman, p. 16 Alan Weintraub/Arcaid,
p. 18–19 Arnaldo Pappalardo/courtesy Instituto Bardi, p. 20 Tuca Reinés,
p. 21 Alan Weintraub/Arcaid, p. 22 Jacob Termansen, pp. 24–25 Jason Schmidt,
pp. 27 courtesy Belmont Freeman, pp. 28–29 Jason Schmidt

Altério Residence, São Paulo, Brazil

Isay Weinfeld, Rua André Fernandes, 175, Itaim-Bibi 04536-020, São Paulo, SP, Brazil,
t: +55.11.3079.7581, f: +55.11.3079.5656, e: projeto@isayweinfeld.com, www.isayweinfeld.com
Designer: Isay Weinfeld; Collaborator: Domingos Pascali; Project manager:
Elena Scarabotolo; Project team: Ana Luisa Pinheiro, Carolina Maluhy, Isis Chaulon;
Photographer: Romulo Fialdini

Casas La Chiripa, Acapulco, Mexico

Felipe Leal, architect, Yucatán 37, Tizapán San Angel, CP 01090 México D.F, Mexico,
t/f: + 52.55.56.16.11.30, e: fleal@ prodigy.net.mx
Principal: Felipe Leal; Collaborators: Antonio Alarcón, Juan Manuel Garibay;
Masonry: Alfredo Fonseca; Ironwork: Frederico Galicia; Engineer: Miguel Garcia;
Structural carpentry: Eusebio Cristóbal; Landscape: Pedro Arizmendi;
Photography: Luis Gordoa, Alberto Moreno Guzmán (p. 45)

Palm Island House, Miami Beach, Florida, USA

Keenen/Riley, 526 West 26th Street, #9A, New York, NY 10001, USA,
t: +1.212.645.9210, f: +1.212.645.9211, e: info@krnyc.com, www.krnyc.com
Architecture and decoration: Keenen/Riley; Project team: John Keenen, Joseph Serrins;
Landscape design: Edwina von Gal; Art consultant: John Keenen; Contractor: Walid Wahab;
Stair fabrication: Aileron; Photographer: William Abranowicz

Taylor House, Scotland Cay, Bahamas

Frank Harmon Architect, 706 Montford Street, Raleigh, North Carolina 27603, USA,
t: +1.919.829.9464, f: +1.919.829.2202
Design principal: Frank Harmon; Design and construction drawings: Quan Banh;
Design and design/build: Vinny Petrarca; Industrial designer: Jim Taylor;
Interior designer: Janice Hocking Taylor; Photographer: James West/JWest Productions

Casa de Crystal, Vieques, Puerto Rico

Henry Myerberg, AIA, Principal, Rockwell Group, 5 Union Square West,
New York, NY 10003, USA, t: +1.212 463 0334, f: +1.212 463 0335, e: hmyerberg@rockwellgroup.com
Principal in charge: Henry Myerberg; Team members: Miguel Jablonski, Alan Wahl, Don
Downie; Structural Engineer: Marcelino Acosta; Contractor: Francisco Cruz Perez;
Photographer: José Jimenez

Casa de Carmen, Rancho Nuevo, Mexico

Leddy Maytum Stacy Architects, 677 Harrison Street, San Francisco, CA 94107, USA,
t: +415.495.1700, f: +415.495.1717, www.lmsarch.com
Principal: Marsha Maytum; Senior associate: Roberto Sheinberg; Project team: Michelle
Huber; Architect of record: TLMS Architects; Construction manager: Rod Bradley; Contractor:
Miguel Garcia Silva; Photographers: Luis Gordoa, Undine Pröhl (pp. 79, 84, 86 [top], 87)

Beach House, Casuarina Beach, Australia

Lahz Nimmo Architects, Level 5, 116–122 Kippax Street, Surry Hills, 2010 NSW, Australia, t: +61.9211.1220, f: +61.9211.1554

Project team: Annabel Lahz, Andrew Nimmo, Peter Titmuss, Tim Horton, Marcus Trimble; Project manager: Steve Marais; Developer: Consolidated Properties; Structural engineer: Murty McKeague; Hydraulics: Ron Goodwin; Landscape designer: Alan Grant Landscape; Interior designer: Lahz Nimmo Architects; Art consultants: Artworkers Alliance; Environmental consultants: Michael Mobbs Sustainable Projects and Design; Pacific Architecture; Builder: Hutchinson Builders; Photographer: Brett Boardman Photography

Sverner Residence, São Paulo, Brazil

Isay Weinfeld

Designer: Isay Weinfeld; Collaborator: Domingos Pascali; Project Manager: Monica Cappa Santoni; Project team: Ana Luisa Pinheiro, Fabio Rudnik, Flavia Oide, Isis Chaulon, Vladimir Navrazini; Photographer: Tuca Reinés

Three Houses by Studio MORSA, Nevis, West Indies

Studio MORSA, 247 Centre Street, New York, NY 10013, USA, t: +1.212.226.4324, f: +1.212.941.9445, e. studiom@att.net

Architects: Antonio Morello, Donato Savoie, RA; Photographer: Antoine Bootz

Weiss Residence, Cabo San Lucas, Mexico

Steven Harris Architects, 50 Warren Street, New York, NY 10007, USA, t: +1.212.587.1108, f: +1.212.385.2932, e: sh@stevenharrisarchitects.com, www.stevenharrisarchitects.com

Architect: Steven Harris; Project manager: Antonio Zaninovic; Design team: Tom Zook; Interior designer: Lucien Rees-Roberts; Landscape designer: Margie Ruddick Landscape; Contractor: Alejandro Trevino Construction; Photographer: Scott Frances/ESTO

Gamma-Issa Residence, São Paulo, Brazil

Márcio Kogan Architecture, Al. Tiete 505, São Paulo, SP, Brazil, t: +55.11.3081.3522, f: +55.11.3063.3424, e: mk-mk@uol.com.br, www.marciokogan.com.br

Designer: Márcio Kogan; Collaborators: Gisela Zilberman, Diana Radomysler; Design team: Bruno Gomes, Cassia Cavani, Oswaldo Pessano; Illumination and security systems: Autoraf Projetos e Instalações Especiais; Structure: Aluízio A.M. D'Avila Engenharia de Projetos; Air conditioning: Arcoplan Planejamento Térmico; Builder: DP Engenharia e Empreendimentos; Photographer: Arnaldo Pappalardo

Figueroa Residence, Miami Beach, Florida, USA

Luis Guillermo Pons, design architect, John R. Medina & Associates, 4901 SW 75th Avenue, Miami, Florida 33155, USA, t. +1.305.740.0554, f. +1.305.740.5355

Design architect: Luis Guillermo Pons; Project manager: Maria T. Moral; Architect of record: John R. Medina, AIA; Builder: Alberto C. Rodriguez; Stonework: Magaly Acosta; Woodworking: Laureano Borges; Metalwok: Jose A. Caceres, Andres L. Ruiz, Luis Bruni; MEP Engineers: Michael C. Guerrero, PE; Rafael L. Gonalez, PE; Structural engineer: Hector de los Reyes; Landscape architecture: Miguel A. Pons, Luis Guillermo Pons, John R. Medina; Photographer: Troy Campbell

Casa Triangular, Vieques, Puerto Rico, USA

John Hix Architect Ltd., RR3, Tottenham, Ontario L0G 1W0, Canada,
t/f: +1.905.729.3364, Info@johnhixarchitect.com, www.johnhixarchitect.com,
c/o Hix Island House, HC-02 Box 14902, Vieques, Puerto Rico 00765, USA,
t/f: +1.787.741.2797
Architecture, planning, and landscape design: John Hix;
Structural engineer: Marcelino Acosta; Contractor: Paco Cruz

Victoria Park House, Singapore

SCDA Architects, 10 Teck Lim Road, Singapore 088386, Singapore,
t: +65.6324.5458, f: +65.6324.5450, e: scda@starhub.net.sg
Architect: Chan Soo Khian; Civil and structural engineer: MSE Engineering & Management
Consultants; Surveyor: J H & Lim; Landscaping: SCDA Architects/Nyee Phoe;
Contractor: Huat Builders; Photographer: Jacob Termansen

Jayawardene House, Mirissa, Sri Lanka

Geoffrey Bawa, architect, c/o The Lunuganga Trust, No.11, 33rd Lane, Off Bagatelle Road
Colombo 3, Sri Lanka, e: leopold@eureka.lk
Architecture and design: Geoffrey Bawa; Design assistants: Murad Ismail, Channa Daswatte;
Engineering: Deepal Wickremasinghe; Photographer: Christian Richters

Sandbank House, Charlotte Amalie, St. Thomas, USVI

William Lane Architects, 350 Lincoln Road, Suite 501, Miami Beach, FL 33139, USA
t: +1.305.531.5292, f: +1.305.531.5494, e: wlarchitects@aol.com
Architect and contractor: William Lane; Structural engineer: Garland Wilson

Bitter Residence, Tijucopava, Brazil

Isay Weinfeld
Designer: Isay Weinfeld; Collaborator: Domingos Pascali; Project manager: Monica Cappa
Santoni; Project team: Fabio Rudnik, Flavia Oide, Isis Chaulon; Photographer: Tuca Reinés

Gold Coast House. Reedy Creek, Australia

Innovarchi, 88 Phillip Street, Sydney 2000 NSW, Australia,
t: +61.2.9247.6191, f: +61.2.9247.6148, www.innovarchi.com
Project team: Stephanie Smith, Ken McBryde, Ben Duckworth, Jad Silvester, Giulietta
Biraghi, Torben Kjaer; Structural engineer: Rod Bligh/Bligh Tanner; Glazing consultant:
John Perry/Hyder Consulting; Builder: Rick Hering; Glazing contractor: Lidco;
Photographer: John Linkins

La Ribereña, Caracas, Venezuela

Original architect: Walter James Alcock; Interior renovation architect: Keenen/Riley;
Project team: John Keenen, Jan Greben; Photographer: Michael Moran

Tropical pages

pp. 30–31, 68–79, 96–97, 122–123, 144–145, 170–171, 198–199, 222 photographs by Claudia Brandenburg
p. 63: Derek Walcott, Nobel laureate, from Nobel awards speech (Literature), 1992
p. 96: Oscar Niemeyer, Brazilian architect, from *Brazil: A Travel Survival Kit* (3rd edition)
p. 145: Arati Chari, "A Language of Spaces," published in URBAN SPACES: August 1, 1999
p. 171: Le Corbusier, from *Towards A New Architecture*
p. 198: Walter James Alcock, Venezuelan architect, from *Alcock: Works and Projects 1959–1992*